T5-BQB-595

Fear in the Countryside:

The Control of Agricultural Resources in the Poor Countries by Nonpeasant Elites

E. G. Vallianatos
Center for Population Studies
Harvard University

Ballinger Publishing Company ● Cambridge, Mass.
A Subsidiary of J.B. Lippincott Company

Robert Manning Strozier Library

FEB 20 1979

Tallahassee, Florida

 This book is printed on recycled paper.

Copyright © 1976 by Ballinger Publishing Company. All rights reserved.
No part of this publication may be reproduced, stored in a retrieval system, or transmitted in any form or by any means, electronic mechanical
photocopy, recording or otherwise, without the prior written consent of
the publisher.

International Standard Book Number: 0-88410-298-X

Library of Congress Catalog Card Number: 76-14355

Printed in the United States of America

Library of Congress Cataloging in Publication Data
Vallianatos, E. G.
  Fear in the countryside.

  Includes bibliographical references.
  1. Food supply. 2. Underdeveloped areas—Agriculture. 3. Technical assistance.
4. Technology transfer. I. Title.
HD9000.6.V28   338.1'9   76-14355
ISBN 0-88410-298-X

To the Small Farmer of this
Small Planet

Contents

List of Tables

List of Figures

Foreword

If one thing has been made clear in the last few years, it is that no intervention is as sure, as easy, as simple, or as controllable as it may have appeared initially. Nor is its success, if indeed success follows, necessarily the kind envisioned by its original sponsors. The Green Revolution of the 1960's, the development and proliferation in the agriculture of the developing nations, of high-yield disease-resistant varieties of wheat and rice, is a good example. By no means as simple an operation as some popular publications made it appear, the Green Revolution has been stalled, at least temporarily, and not only by the astronomical rise in the cost of fuel, fertilizer, and agricultural chemicals brought on by the quadrupling of oil prices by the OPEC nations in 1973–74.

The Green Revolution, in reality, was never merely a genetic breakthrough: to be permanently successful, it also demands a profound technological revolution if developing nations are to become self-sufficient in food production. The green-revolution varieties of grain produce high yields only with good irrigation (requiring wells, canals, and oil-run pumps) and large amounts of high-nitrogen, oil-based fertilizers. Water and fertilizer also produce more weeds, which require more herbicides. A larger crop requires more pesticides in the field, more silos for storage, more fungicides and rodenticides to protect the stored crop, more trucks to transport farm input and output, and more roads for the trucks. The investment in seeds, chemicals, and equipment requires a system of rural credit, a good agricultural-research establishment, and a good extension service to assist the subsistence farmer suddenly turned businessman. In many communities, literacy training is necessary if the farmer is to read the instructions on potentially-lethal agricultural chemicals. In short, the Green Revolution has presupposed the presence of a Western-style agricultural economy.

All too often, then, in nations whose social and economic structure has traditionally placed control of wealth and land in the hands of a small, ruling elite, the Green Revolution, while it has contributed larger (and desperately needed) crops, has also contributed to the expansion of large farms and the wealth of large landowners at the expense of marginal, subsistence farmers. Farm mechanization has displaced landless laborers. The tragic result is, the influx of ill-educated, untrained, jobless workers from rural areas to those bulging shantytowns that grow like cancers around the large cities, where, still jobless, millions live in disease and poverty.

Among many people concerned with the precarious world food situation, there tend to be two opposing camps or schools of thought. Economists and agriculturalists argue that if we can only stimulate the economy sufficiently and produce more food, all will be well. Social reformers, on the other hand, reply that what is needed is not so much more food and a high GNP as much better distribution of available resources. Both these positions, I believe, are a return to the simplistic solutions of a few years ago. In fact, we must have higher food production *and* greater distributive justice if we are to feed the world. We cannot reject the new grain varieties for, in the short run, say the next twenty years or so, they are our only sure bulwark against massive famines. But we must also get this food to all, and that means a decent income for all. That this can be done, if a government cares enough, is evident from the recent history of a number of very different Asian societies: Taiwan, Hongkong, Singapore, Mainland China, North and South Korea. It has become clear, however, that in the short or medium run, at least, it cannot be done simply by a massive infusion of Western agricultural technology and certainly not by massive Western-style industrial growth at the expense of the agricultural sector.

What is needed is local variations of the Green Revolution: the development of basic and applied agricultural research leading to intermediary technologies that will increase crop productivity for sufficient food and maintain crop variety for good nutrition within the context of a mainly tropical, high labor-intensive, comparatively unsophisticated agriculture. Only thus will rising incomes place a firm economic base under rural communities. It is to this problem that Dr. Vallianatos has addressed himself. His thoughts should be of help to economists and planners, and of interest to every concerned reader.

Dr. Jean Mayer
Professor of Nutrition
Harvard University

5/4/76

Preface

No one could affirm that this book is an objective account of the present situation of world agriculture or of the prospects for the future. It is instead a manifesto—a book of passionate advocacy, which argues eloquently for the necessity of improving the conditions of life of the world's poorest billion, the "small farmers" and landless agricultural laborers of the earth's poor countries. It documents the inequalities and injustices that are suffered by the rural poor and the desperation of their struggle for survival against handicaps created not by nature, but by their fellow men.

The author is neither a natural scientist nor an economist, but a historian, and he has been able to bring some of the insights of his discipline to bear on the world food problem—a historian's consciousness of the complexity of human affairs, the importance of the unequal distribution of political and social power, the blindness of the rich and powerful toward the needs of the poor and weak, and their capacity to exploit their fellow human beings for their own interests.

He shows that in their reactions to the possibilities of agricultural improvement through the application of modern science and technology, the behavior of poor farmers everywhere is governed as much by their fear of failure as by the prospects for increased production. The economist calls this behavior risk-aversion. The historian describes the reality that the poor farmer on his tiny plot of land, often with a burden of perpetual indebtedness and with a growing family to feed, is barely able to grow enough food for himself and his dependents, even in good years. The peasant believes he cannot take a chance on new methods that have not been tested by his own experience. More significantly, his farming is a system on a micro scale, in which all the resources of his family, his animals, and his meagre stock of tools are used to produce a diversity of food supplies, mostly for consumption within the household, not only a mixture of cereals and other staples, but also vitamin-containing green vegetables and milk or other animal products. He must balance the safety of diversity against the vastly increased production that could be obtained by concentrating on one crop at a time, using modern high-yielding, fertilizer and water-demanding crop varieties. Unless there is an adequate infrastructure of inexpensive transportation, stable water supplies, equitable marketing arrangements, credit on fair terms, security of land tenure, and prices for his farm products that more than balance the costs of fertilizers, irrigation water and other purchased inputs, the small farmer has little reason to change his traditional ways.

I find much in this book with which I disagree. Many statements appear overdrawn or one-sided, but I cannot disagree with the basic thesis that the challenge to our humanity in the rich countries is the help lift the burden of poverty and misery from the backs of the majority of mankind, the rural poor. This is a task that will demand greater intellectual effort and a higher level of moral courage than has yet been witnessed.

Roger Revelle,
   Richard Saltonstall Professor of Population Policy
Harvard Center for Population Studies

and Professor of Science and Public Policy
University of California at San Diego

Acknowledgments

I am grateful to Werner Kiene and Refugio I. Rochin for both encouragement and sound advice. Max Milner, Richard Gilmore, Sterling Wortman, Barbara H. Tuckman, David Pimentel, Richard Levins, and Pierre R. Crosson read the manuscript in part or in whole and their comments were of considerable profit to this work. I am also profoundly thankful to Roger Revelle and Jean Mayer for their unfailingly perceptive judgements on my work both at its inception and during its evolution. Their advice mixed approbation, criticism, and suggestion in optimum proportions. The counsel and wisdom of Everett Mendelsohn and of my friend Lindsay Mattison did much to prepare me for this work. My protracted dialogue and interaction with a few of the underdeveloped country scientists at the Harvard Center for Population Studies were enormously helpful in grasping at some of the intellectual and social underpinnings of backwardness and development. Lest it be forgotten, it is appropriate to stress that in no way whatsoever should the interpretations of this work be taken to mean that they reflect the development position of the Harvard Center for Population Studies or the ideas of this book's critics. It would also be erroneous and misleading to assume that those who endorsed this book are somehow burdened to defend its findings and recommendations. I remain solely responsible for the book as it is.

E. G. Vallianatos

Harvard University
November 1975

Fear in the Countryside

 *Introduction*

The Critical and
Global Food Imperative

AGRICULTURE AND MATERIAL LIFE

Man has always had a food problem. The birth of agriculture
did not solve that problem. It simply made man's existence
in relation to sufficient food supplies less precarious. Agriculture has been a way of life for the majority of mankind for
thousands of years. The cultivation of wheat, rice, and corn and the
domestication of animals were at the root of man's evolving material
civilization. Agriculture instructed each new generation in survival by
handing down elementary tools, empirical processes, and enough
knowledge to assure that life was not completely static. New knowledge has for centuries helped the farmer to improve his capabilities in
raising food. In time, wild species of plants were replaced by cultivated
and more productive varieties. Hybridization was responsible for the
improvement of corn as a foodcrop; and the domestication of animals
gave the farmer a reliable source of meat, skins, and draft work.
Irrigation, crop rotation, and the use of manures were fundamental
tools that transformed agriculture. Such a transformation has been a
dynamic process, involving as it does continuous innovation and self-
renewal.

Man started to hunt animals at the end of the Paleolithic Age.
Several thousand years later he introduced cultivated cereals to his
daily diet, thus balancing his need to hunt or to raise an extensive
stock. But since it was much easier to cultivate cereals they soon
became the daily meal of the vast majority of men. Meat eating distinguished the rich from the poor who fed on bread, gruel, roots, and

cooked tubers. With very little pasture land the Asiatic rice-growing civilizations never had to choose between cereals and meat. The Europeans chose to be carnivorous down to the seventeenth century simply because their countryside provided vast lands for pasturing animals. The rapid population growth that followed the scientific revolution of the seventeenth century forced the Europeans to eat less meat and more cereals. Only the introduction of scientific stock-raising and the arrival of meat from America in the middle of the nineteenth century enabled Europe to satisfy its appetite for meat.

The birth of agriculture helped man to increase his food supplies but it did not eliminate famine. Whether catastrophic reductions in food supplies are due to natural disasters or are manmade, the resulting famine is equally catastrophic to human communities. In 1064 famine hit Egypt:

> For seven successive years the overflow of the Nile failed, and with it almost the entire subsistence of the country; while the rebels interrupted supplies of grain from the north. Two provinces were entirely depopulated; in another half the inhabitants perished; while in Cairo city (El-Kahvich), the people were reduced to the direst straits. Bread was sold for 14 dirhems to the loaf; and all provisions being exhausted, the worst horrors of famine followed. The wretched resorted to cannibalism, and organised bands kidnapped the unwary passenger in the desolate streets, principally by means of ropes furnished with hooks and let down from the latticed windows.

In 1068–1069 England experienced famine. Men sold themselves into slavery, ate dogs and horses, and even resorted to cannibalism. For nine years a great part of England lay waste without inhabitants.[1] In the Indian famine of 1769–1770 about three million people perished: "The air was so infected by the noxious effluvia of dead bodies, that it was scarcely possible to stir abroad without perceiving it; and without hearing also the frantic cries of the victims of famine who were seen at every stage of suffering and death. Whole families expired, and villages were desolated." Again, India had another famine in 1790–1791: "So great was the distress that many people fled to other districts in search of food; while others destroyed themselves, and some killed their children, and lived on their flesh."[2] Such have been the horrors of human communities in hunger.

HUMAN ECOLOGY OF RESOURCE USE

For the novice ours is an age of paradoxes. Writing in 1963, a group of Americans engaged in large-scale international philanthropy and technical assistance said that:

About half of the human beings on earth have an inadequate diet, and millions live constantly on the edge of starvation, despite the fact that an overabundance of food is produced in a few technologically advanced countries. A world which possesses the knowledge and methods to confront the demands of hunger must accelerate its efforts to increase the production and improve the distribution of food supplies.[3]

At the present juncture of history the most pressing of human needs is an adequate food supply:

> Food supply is not merely a matter of the number of bushels of grain the farmer harvests or the number of chickens he raises. Other vital elements in the equation are the selection, handling, processing, storage, transportation and marketing of the food crops. Each factor allows opportunities for improvement of efficiency that can greatly enhance the food supply.[4]

Considering the grim facts of world food production for just 1972, it is easy to see the enormity of the human predicament in the context of those millions of people who simply do not have enough food to eat:

> Inadequate rain cut the 1972 Soviet grain crop, while drought in Argentina and Australia crippled grain production. . . . India's monsoon dropped below normal, cutting the cereal crop and eroding hopes for near-term self-sufficiency in cereal production. Peru's fish catch was a disaster; drought and typhoons slashed rice and corn crops in the Philippines; and, in the United States the corn and soybean harvest was stalled by wet weather in the fall of 1972.[5]

But neither the United States nor the Soviet Union are likely to go hungry. They and the rest of the affluent one billion people dominate the world food market. They also feed their livestock[6] as much cereal as the two billion citizens of the less developed nations use for food. It is also unlikely that the food gap between the rich and the poor countries will be bridged soon. Even with increases in farm production and income and a lowering of population growth, the two billion poor will be "inadequately fed for decades to come."[7]

The present food crisis is part of a broad ecological and social problem of global dimensions. It mirrors the failure of modern technological civilization to give man not merely material goods but what he needs most, namely a sense of purpose to satisfy the human spirit:

> Modern civilization has reached the stage where, henceforth, no new use of technology, no increased demands on the environment for food, for other natural resources, for areas to be used for recreation, or for places

to store the debris of civilization, can be undertaken to benefit some groups of individuals without a high risk of injury to others.[8]

Man must choose in his use of natural resources. Space on this planet, water, or environmental quality may become the limiting resources for man. In prehistoric times resources at man's command were extremely limited. The cave man used the forest and the wild kingdom. Those were the only resources available to him. There is no relation between population and resources except in a historical, accidental way. India and China have had large populations because they have had rich land. It takes a lot of water to grow food. Large regions of the earth have or do not have water supplies. South America has more water than it actually needs. Water is very unevenly distributed and by necessity lack of water becomes a limiting factor.

Technological civilization is based on energy. In the poor countries the energy the peasant gets out of his farm he uses for his sole survival. Energy has been abundant in the United States because it has been inexpensive. However, this inexpensive energy policy is not likely to continue for long in the United States:

the days of a free energy market—if such ever existed—are over . . . balancing this country's energy budget will be a tougher job than putting a man on the moon. The Manhattan Project and Project Apollo do indeed seem relatively simple compared with the national energy challenge, for they were aimed at quite specific technological goals. . . . *Once energy is held at a premium in society, it forces a profound reordering of social and economic values.* (Emphasis mine.)[9]

Historically, man has used wood, water power, coal, and petroleum and natural gas for energy. He now has nuclear fission and geothermal and solar energy as possible sources of energy. Nuclear fission breaks up the atoms to smaller units. It is used in atomic power plants to supply electrical power. In nuclear fusion light elements combine to form heavier ones in the presence of several million degrees of temperature. This nuclear reaction is potentially the source of unlimited energy but it is still in the experimental stage. Geothermal energy is very limited in its geographical distribution. Solar energy is the greatest, the only unlimited energy source. But solar energy is diffuse. This poses difficult problems in concentrating, storing, and converting it to electricity. Wind is a form of energy originating in solar radiation.

It is not laziness but survival needs that create the apparent apathy of those millions of the poor in the underdeveloped nations. Lack of food destroys the ability for physical activity of millions of adults in the poor countries. Survival demands inactivity. The food that people eat depends on their size, physical activity, and gender. A child eats more than an adult simply because he is more active. An old man eats very little: "An old man is no burden in the house since he demands no more food than a baby."[10] Body size depends on food intake. There is also a racial, genetic correlation between restricted diet and body size. Adequate diet for the people of the poor countries will require an increase of food supply in the future. From cereals alone 2,900 kilocalories are available per person per day. The poorest in the poor nations receive far less than their physiological requirements. The poor countries produce less than half of the world food supply. *Maldistribution is the most crucial problem in the food supply of the earth.* The increasing consumption of meat in the rich countries and the rapid population growth in the poor countries have made food a critical problem.

An equally critical problem to both the rich and the poor countries is the continuing environmental degradation. Changing technologies, demand on resources for economic growth, and population increases have given birth to the environmental crisis. Modern economic man without a collective memory or respect for history has in the last two centuries plundered and poisoned the environment, thereby reaching the turning point for his own destruction. Scarcity of renewable resources and scientific evidence demonstrate that there is a definite limit to the amount of debris that the earth, sea, and biosphere can absorb. The affluent generate the most per capita waste, building cities with tremendous waste disposal problems. The pollution of the rich countries has very little to do with the problem of population increase. The environmental problems of the underdeveloped nations are those of poverty. For example, forests are destroyed in highly populated areas for rice cultivation and for energy; or, the poor condition of intestinal lining caused by worms and amoebas makes digestion of food difficult, which in turn means that a lot of food is wasted; or, infected water supplies carry and spread diseases in a geometric rate.

It is difficult to estimate the costs of pollution. The environment has different uses for different people. This makes an economic analysis of the environment a doubtful proposition. Many resources are common property. Some parts of the environment are literally irreplaceable. They are priceless. The environmental problem is primarily a political, an ethical, and an economic problem.

We need to preserve diversity in nature. We have to think of our inheritance as a precious commodity. Like our intellectual ancestors the Greeks, we must feel in harmony with the natural world. To improve environmental quality we must have enough knowledge to predict. Predictability of the effects of change is important. Science can show man his place in nature. This means we must know more about ecology.[11] The sciences, both natural and social, are necessary to instruct man on ecological principles. Social institutions and mechanisms are also needed to guard the public interest. "What is to be done" must always be in our sight. This is a question of values, or morality. We can be neither give-up pessimists nor sit-back optimists in the future. We must be workers. Commitment is essential for a better tomorrow.

If the ecological crisis is permitted to run its course, not only will it destroy humanity but, even before that catastrophe arrives, the underdeveloped world will more likely than not take the issue upon itself and demand more resources from the advanced industrialized world. It is neither easy nor wise to speculate about such a confrontation. But what seems to be certain is that, given the immense disparity of wealth between the highly industrialized West and the low-income nations, the causes of democracy and freedom are likely to continue to be the first victims of such social inequality of global dimensions. The emergence of tyranny has always been associated with social crises, but tyranny itself has never managed to solve the problems that brought it to power. Hence, the knowledge-producing nations have vital responsibilities to contribute freely their technological know-how to assist the poor nations to modernize their agricultural potential along lines fitting their ecological and human resources.

The first step in closing the gap between the rich nations and the poor nations is to transfer enough knowledge, including agricultural science and technology, to those with precarious food supplies so that they can in time eliminate hunger and break the chains of poverty. This argument is not new. The experience of Japan in modernizing its agriculture by the intelligent use of Western science and technology suffices to show that the transfer of knowledge from one civilization to another is possible. Greece won political independence in the 1820s from Ottoman rule precisely because the transfer of Western knowledge prepared her to experience an intellectual revolution before a political revolution. Writing in 1803, the Greek social thinker and educational philosopher Adamantios Koraes (1748–1833) said:

> it is easier to transmit knowledge from one country to another than to transport their respective products and staples. And in fact for some years now the Greeks have added the commerce of science to their ordinary trade. From all over Europe, and particularly from France, they import books and knowledge just as they import cloth, metalwork, and other products of European industry.[12]

It may also be pertinent here to recall that every developed society of today was sometime in its past an underdeveloped society. The United States "received at birth a maximum transfer of the driving ideas and generative economic and political institutions" of the European society:[13]

> from the beginning, Americans have participated in cultural relations and development, first as consumers, then as producers of transferable ideas and institutions. We are characterized . . . as one of the early developing nations who received, sifted, and adapted a cultural heritage for which others had paid the price. Moreover, the transfer took place on American soil as Englishmen, Frenchmen, Spaniards, and many others shared their arts and letters, religion and constitutionalism.[14]

Agricultural production depends on land, seed, fertilizer, water, energy, material capital, and farmers. And agricultural science and technology are the significant components of the material capital of modern agriculture. Each society possesses these factors but has employed them in an infinite variety. This fact explains why it has always been that certain communities have rarely experienced hunger while others lived constantly in fear of famine. Differences in land are the least important explanatory framework of the different levels of agricultural production and wealth among various human communities. In Latin America, Chile and Argentina, with renowned quality lands, have a stagnant agriculture. In Asia, Japan experienced a sustained increase in agricultural production; and India, with more fertile land, has had a great deal of trouble feeding its own people. It appears that it is not land, but land distribution, the quality of the material capital, who benefits from knowledge, and the skills and dedication of the farmers that make the difference between plenty of food or starvation and stagnant productivity in agriculture. Yet any assistance to the poor countries must strive to eliminate the human-degrading values of technological civilization.[15] Economic efficiency and the taming of nature must not be permitted to flourish at the expense of the cultivation of man or the preservation of nature.

SOCIAL ROOTS OF SCIENCE

The transfer of science and technology to the underdeveloped nations has had a modernizing impact of diverse implications for the future of the people involved. No doubt new knowledge brought the benefits of Western civilization to many of the citizens of the poor countries. But

the carelessness and speed with which this new knowledge was transferred and transplanted in the basically non-Western cultural environment of the underdeveloped nations has, for the most part, had a
devastating effect on the ecological balance of vast regions of the
planet.[16] This is not to say that the ecological damage associated with
the technological development of the poor nations has mainly been
brought by those knowledge-borrowing countries. Part of the blame
has to be shared by the technology-exporting nations. The underdeveloped countries are the least qualified to stem or understand ecological mismanagement.

Human survival will depend largely on man's ability to shape his
technology to the environment. This is to say that man has finally to
define knowledge in terms relevant to the public and global good:

> The inequalities between have and have-not peoples may . . . be viewed
> as a grave threat to the overall future maintenance of the human com-
> munity. The explosive rises in population, the pressures on food lands
> and other resources, the scale of wastage, disorganization, and pestilence
> accompanying our "local" wars are also directly linked to the global
> revolution in human expectation. As physical and psychic events, these
> press even more critically upon the resources and social energies of even
> the so-called advanced nations; as world problems, they are increasingly
> beyond the capacity of any locally organized effort to mitigate, or solve,
> them in anything but the shortest range. . . . We have reached the
> point in human affairs at which the basic ecological requirements for
> sustaining the world community must take precedence over, and be
> superogative to, the more transient value systems and vested interests of
> any local society.[17]

Francis Bacon provided the ethos of the scientific revolution with
the ancient idea that man pursues knowledge for the achievement of
all things possible. A basic question to be raised in considering the
social implications of scientific knowledge is "For whose benefit does
any scientific project take place?" *Science is socially constructed.* It is
important to know where the foci of knowledge in a particular society
are located since the position of the intellectual elite will determine
the kind of knowledge disseminated in that society. *Science is also the
ideology of the class in power.* It, moreover, is a potent means of exploiting nature. It provides an intellectual home for the testing of experience
and, in that capacity, science is a major challenge to establish authority.

As science in the seventeenth century was the counterculture of
European civilization, today science is the counterculture of the civilization of the poor nations:

What I object to [wrote Mahatma Gandhi] is the craze for machinery, not machinery as such. The craze is for what they call labour-saving machinery. Men go on "saving labour" till thousands are without work and thrown on the streets to die of starvation. I want to save time and labour, not for a fraction of mankind, but for all. I want the concentration of wealth, not in the hands of a few, but in the hands of all. Today machinery helps a few to ride on the backs of millions. The impetus behind it is not the philanthropy to save labour, but greed.[18]

But while Western civilization managed to assimilate and naturalize the new scientific knowledge, the underdeveloped nations have had neither the traditions nor the economies to afford the price of naturalizing an essentially foreign body of knowledge into their traditions and culture. For many non-Westerners, European science and technology were simply the diabolical contrivances of the unbelievers:

They scented in them half consciously the coming of a new world, mysterious, pregnant with alarming possibilities, hostile to them because [it was] incompatible with their old world, in which they and their ancestors have lived, secure in their faith, untroubled in their beliefs and prejudices. They saw this new world coming, and had the first premonition that their old world, which they had hitherto thought eternal, would soon begin to slip away from under their feet.[19]

The underdeveloped societies are facing the problems of modernization. They are seeking to transform themselves from an agrarian and rural existence to that of an industrial and urban life. To date, the results of this transformation have not been very encouraging. On April 14, 1972, in an address to the Third United Nations Conference on Trade and Development, Robert S. McNamara, president of the World Bank, said:

The state of development in most of the developing world today is unacceptable. The improvement of the individual lives of the great masses of people is, in the end, what development is all about. What are we to say of a world in which hundreds of millions of people are not only poor in statistical terms, but are faced with day-to-day deprivations that degrade human dignity to levels which no statistics can adequately describe?

—A developing world in which children under age five account for only 20 per cent of the population, but for more than 60 per cent of the deaths.
—A developing world in which two thirds of the children who have

escaped death will live on, restricted in their growth by malnutrition—a malnutrition that can stunt both bodies and minds alike.

—A developing world in which there are 100 million more adult illiterates than there were 20 years ago.

—A developing world, in short, in which death and disease are rampant, education and employment scarce, squalor and stagnation common, and opportunity and the realization of personal potential drastically limited.[20]

One of the keys to modernization has been the availability of knowledge, especially scientific knowledge, for rational decision making. The borrowing of scientific knowledge and technique from the Western world will in the end determine the national development of the less developed countries:

> The first step toward a human future is the acceptance of responsibility for meeting the emergency in our total environment by creating those generalized human conditions which will at least prevent the system from degenerating further. In the immediate term, the only way we know how to do this is by devoting the necessary physical resources to feed the hungry; in the mediate terms, we must do it by inventing the necessary means to graft our technological knowledge on all the branches of the human tree.[21]

COLONIAL THEORY OF BACKWARDNESS

The abject poverty of the great majority of the world's population living in the underdeveloped countries is not fundamentally different from what it was in the nineteenth century. It was in the nineteenth century that Western civilization invaded the native cultures of the poor, non-Western regions of the globe. The colonial experience demonstrated the bankruptcy of imperialism. The exploited might have been convinced that his master was beneficent, enlightened, and cultivated but in the end he found out that he was not permitted to become civilized enough to demand control of his own home. The exploited also learned that he had to pay a terrible price for his discovery that material progress had a somehow uplifting effect on his life. He witnessed the disruption of his culture. And to his horror he realized that Western civilization was incapable of sustaining those who had lost secure values and traditions.

Colonialism gave birth to a theory of backwardness that was intended to relieve the Europeans of moral responsibility for the poverty of their colonies. It was believed that the natives' tendency toward idleness, inefficiency, and restricted economic activity was an unchangeable component of their social and religious institutions and traditions. Climate was also seen as a major reason for low productivity and work inefficiency. To these beliefs the idea was added that non-Western people were not as well endowed as their European masters. Racial inferiority was a logical step from this last hypothesis.

TIME LAG

Clearly this theory of backwardness was apologetic and certainly not flattering to the indigenous millions of people of these regions. When these regions became independent countries, their elites rejected the colonial theory of backwardness. Meanwhile both Soviet-led and United States-led nations began courting these newly emerged poor countries. And since to abandon the colonial theory was one way to balance Communist influence in the former European colonies, the Western developed countries not only gave up that theory quickly but they developed a new one that had none of the offensive implications of the white man's burden. This essentially meant a reinterpretation of backwardness at the expense of unpleasant facts. Neither the ruling poor country elites nor the anxious and diplomatic Western development specialists wanted to talk about colonialism, social institutions, social structures, or climate. Rapid and effective development was assumed to be possible if only the poor countries and their Western-educated elites followed Western models of economic development. It so happened that Western economic theory abstracted from most of the unpleasant elements of the colonial theory. It also abstracted from the very conditions that are responsible for the underdevelopment of the poor countries. By eliminating the importance of climate, especially in the tropics and subtropics, the role of social organizations and institutions, and the effects of income and levels of living, Western economic theory led the poor countries to believe that they only had to close a "time lag" to catch up with the West. This was no more than Marxism, but in the West such a fact was concealed and simplified by the theories of "stages of growth." In this sense the poor countries were fed a one-dimensional development process which was teleologically optimistic.[22]

NEW BACKWARDNESS

The major consequence of this theory of development or new backwardness was the criminal neglect of agriculture in the underdeveloped countries. The price for those countries' reliance on the econometric wizardry of their own Western-educated economists is indeed enormous. In terms of nutrition, literacy, and health the citizen of a developed country enjoys wealth that simply transcends the imagination of the one billion of the poorest of the poor with income less than $200 per year. "His caloric intake is 40 percent greater; his literacy rate is four times higher; the mortality rate of his children is 90 percent lower; and his own life expectancy is 50 percent longer."[23] As if this crushing poverty were not sufficient, the underdeveloped countries until quite recently had few technological resources to upgrade their agriculture. The colonial policy of transferring Western agricultural technology to tropical and subtropical regions in order to improve the cash crops outlived the colonial empires in their political setting. Until the midsixties agricultural technology in the poor countries, if it existed at all, was "Western-based scientific technology" and was strictly confined to export and industrial crops.[24] The decade of the sixties was remarkable if for no other reason than that it postponed the day that the world food problem would be called a "crisis." During the 1960s Western philanthropy and ingenuity brought to maturity foodcrop technologies that for a while met the growing food needs of the world's poor. With considerable optimism and not a little faith in the "new" technological innovations, those responsible for their diffusion and spread announced that the world was witnessing nothing short of a "green revolution." The green revolution, then, could not have come at a more propitious time. But in addition to increasing foodcrop yields, the green revolution initiated the international transfer of agricultural science and technology for the benefit of the poor countries. The green revolution, its institutionalization in a series of research centers, and the transfer of the technologies generated at these institutes have for the most part been the responsibility of the American agricultural technical assistance elite.

TECHNOLOGY TRANSFER AND DEVELOPMENT

Given the record of agricultural technology transfer during the period of colonialism, the very use of the term "technology transfer" is not always proper since "it perpetuates Western technological dominance" over those who import that knowledge.[25] The same idea has been put even more forcefully: "I am very interested in the problem which is usually described in the industrial countries as technology transfer but which I see more as the problem of a science of one's own versus intellectual colonialism, a social more than a technical question."[26]

This thesis cannot easily be challenged. There is no doubt whatsoever that technology transfer is "a social more than a technical question." This is the thesis of this book. The fact that continuous dependence on others for technology leads to intellectual colonialism also needs no documentation. In this context, then, the use of the term "technology transfer" in this essay must be understood to mean the actual transfer of agricultural technologies from the international agricultural research centers to the national research systems and to the farmers of the poor countries. Intellectual colonialism is definitely *not* implied by the use of this term. Technology transfer is part of this book's overall concern with development: "I understand development as the movement upward of the whole social system. In other words, not only production, distribution of the produce, and modes of production are involved, but also levels of livings, institutions, attitudes, and policies."[27] Moreover, this study's thesis cannot be understood outside the context of the following definition of development:

> Development is not just economics or sociology or technology but history. How it proceeds depends to a large extent on how power is distributed among different social groups. The immediate outlook for most of the rural poor in the developing countries is for continued poverty and increased repression. This problem is not going to be solved merely by greater investments in technological improvements of the green revolution or by more abundant credit and technical assistance. Rural development for the low-income majorities requires fundamental and often revolutionary reforms in social institutions.[28]

At this point it is appropriate that the thesis of this book be carefully defined. In no uncertain terms this thesis advances the proposition that the transfer of agricultural technologies to the underdeveloped countries has rarely been successful because of forbidden constraints:

1. Agricultural technologies developed in the temperate zone cannot be transferred to the tropical or subtropical environment primarily because of the biological specificity of plant and animal life. Specific scientific methodology and very specific technical knowledge can be transferred with minimum if any positive application. Only broad scientific knowledge and results may have a beneficial impact on a different foodcrop context, provided the technologies they represent are elaborated and particularized.
2. The transfer of agricultural technologies to the poor countries must necessarily involve a continuous adaptation and acceptance of each new technology to major or minor physical and social

niches. This means that a lot of technology transfer never takes place.

3. Technology adaptation is a costly process. It is also a scientifically taxing exercise that is beyond the indigenous research capability of underdeveloped countries.

4. The technological and biological components of agricultural technologies make such technologies sensitive to soil, climate, wealth, and poverty; and like technology generation, technology adaptation serves the interests of its creators.

5. The green revolution was an experiment in technology adaptation. Financed as it was by rich and poor country elites, the green revolution adapted technologies to the resource parameters of the underdeveloped country large landowners.

6. The poverty-stricken, elite-ridden rural economies of the underdeveloped world have land tenure arrangements that by their gross inequalities determine not merely rural income distribution but the distribution of technologies.

7. Agricultural technology transfer is an exceedingly complex technological and social process. Involving as it does the generation, export, adaptation, and dissemination of expensive knowledge, it reaches only those with adequate resources; and in the poor countries it is not the small farmer who can afford such knowledge.

8. New technologies will benefit those who till the soil of resource-scarcity agriculture only when such technologies are developed within the context of labor-intensive agricultural economies based on the institutional, technological, and social arrangements favoring the peasant farmer.

9. In small farm agriculture, technologies must relate water use and management to multiple cropping. And technologies have to be developed to integrate crops and livestock, to accommodate changes in cropping patterns in irrigated and rainfed land in order to optimize income and employment and to benefit productive systems of foodcrops, livestock, and nonfood forage crops.

10. The peasant farmer is the backbone and victim of both economy and poverty in the underdeveloped countries. He produces most of the food of his society. Yet that same society has institutions that provide the small farmer neither credit nor fertile land or public services so freely available to the prosperous producers.

What are the limitations of this thesis? Clearly the transfer of agricultural technologies to those countries that have institutionalized inequalities will not reduce but widen the gap between the affluent and poor farmer. This is precisely the case in Latin America. My thesis, at least in its social dimensions, loses some of its force in the context of the Asian and African experience not so much because of the absence of social inequalities in those continents but because of the constraints governing the secondary information sources used to some degree in the writing of this book.

PERMANENT FAMINE FOR THE WORLD'S POOR

In 1972 the United States kept 40 million acres of farmland fallow. During the same year disastrous weather created a food situation where for the first time in 25 years world production of cereals fell by 33 million tons. At the same time global cereal prices rose in 1972. The following year the price of petroleum increased to the point that the whole supply of fertilizers and energy for the poor countries became and continues to be at best problematic and extremely precarious. Meanwhile rapid population growth in the underdeveloped countries continues to add millions of people per year to the hundreds of millions of the poor suffering from significant undernutrition and/or starvation. Starvation wastes and kills. It is a ghastly process whereby the human body burns itself out sometimes thoroughly and sometimes partially, but perhaps with permanent ill effects on mental development. Inadequate intake of energy and/or protein, happening as it does over long periods of time among the poor in the poor regions of the earth, results in apathy, emaciation, weight loss, and the physical and mental deterioration of those who fall victims to kwashiorkor and marasmus. Malnutrition problems and diseases are also interrelated to the absence of certain nutrients from the food the poor eat. In the Far East vitamin A deficiency is responsible for the blindness of more than 100,000 children annually.

Food has always been the most vital and critical commodity for the survival and welfare of mankind. The genesis of the world food problem preceded the 1972 sharp decline of food production. Its roots are imbedded in a global rapid population growth, global maldistribution of resources, and gross social and economic inequalities in the poor countries. It is the underdeveloped countries with the lowest per capita income, the highest birth rates, and subsistence food economies that for a long time to come will be unable to meet their food needs. But the world food problem has also become a critical problem for the resource-rich countries like the United States. Rich societies cannot survive for long in an ocean of poverty and hunger.

The industrial societies of the West and Japan are no more than one-quarter of the world's population, yet they command three-quarters of the total global resources in capital and technology. This privileged minority also spends about $30 billion in order to protect its farmers. At the same time the societies of the underdeveloped countries, burdened as they are by near stagnant economies, are facing the grim prospect of total collapse. The most formidable constraint inhibiting the poor countries' efforts to redress their poverty is poverty itself. Within the borders of the underdeveloped world, a billion or so of hungry humanity has lost much of a chance for a decent future. The 1974 lavish international Bucharest and Rome receptions on population and food may indicate that the world community has perhaps abandoned mass starvation as a solution to the problem of too many poor people with very little food. The dying peasant of Bangladesh is still dying. And the cold, global silence since the elites of the poor and the rich got together to discuss population and food in 1974 offers little comfort that those with technology and resources and those who govern the poor have managed to transcend their priorities to worry only about their slice of bread.[29] That the green revolution failed to stay green has at least brought to an end the flood of panegyrics[30] celebrating a revolution that was never a scientific or social revolution and much less a revolution designed to benefit the poor. It is sobering if bitter to learn that the underdeveloped world is at a state of "permanent famine"[31] and that malnutrition is "primarily a manifestation of social injustice."[32]

THE QUESTION OF TECHNOLOGY AND THE SMALL PEASANT FARMER

It has been argued that "[t]he modernization of agriculture depends on overall social and economic development in the poor countries as well as on the development and dissemination of new knowledge to the farmers."[33] It can also be said that agriculture is "an overwhelmingly important component" of the poor country's economy and that agricultural modernization in the underdeveloped regions of the world "is one of the great challenges facing mankind." Since modernization is almost synonymous with the uses of science and technology, it is pertinent here to add that science and technology can have a wide beneficial impact "only in the context of changes in social and economic institutions."[34] It is in this broad philosophical understanding of development that I wrote this book. I also wanted to bring out with all the discernment at my command the social implications of the introduction of the high-yielding foodcrop technologies of the 1960s to the tropical political economies of the underdeveloped countries. The whole study was conceived and executed in the context of what appears to be a very simple question: Do existing agricultural technologies reach the small peasant farmer in the poor countries? The pages that follow will demonstrate that the small farmer question is not simple at all. In fact it will be shown that this question is likely to become the question of the next century. This is not because somehow intellectuals will suddenly "discover" the peasant. The peasant and the intellectual have co-existed for centuries. The fact is that the peasant, be he a small farmer, landless agricultural worker, or sharecropper, constitutes the majority within the rural majorities of the population in the nonindustrialized poor countries. It is clear then that the future of the peasant farmer is in a real sense the future of three-quarters of the human population. Again, do technologies or new knowledge reach the small peasant farmer of the low-income countries? Those who finance and continue to develop more and more "new green revolution technologies" answer this question in the affirmative. Theirs is a very difficult position to challenge. They have statistics, a sophisticated public relations information system, impressive laboratories, and abundant wealth to dazzle the observer. Besides, accessibility to the green revolution peasant is not easy outside the context of the green revolution establishment.

I wrote parts of this book in the splendid isolation that Harvard University provides from agricultural and especially rural problems. I met and talked to some of the architects of the green revolution in the New York offices of the Rockefeller and Ford foundations. I read their writings. And despite my critical attitude I absorbed some of their thinking. This left me disturbed. The world food problem was getting worse every day. I could not balance that grim reality with the glowing success stories of the green revolution. I resolved that dilemma by visiting Colombia during August 1975. In Colombia I talked to several members of the ruling and agricultural elites. I traveled widely, especially in the mountainous province of Garcia Rovira and in the prosperous Valle del Cauca. But above all I spent most of my time with small farmers. International agricultural scientists working in Colombia, Colombian intellectuals, scientists, and small farmers spoke to me freely and frankly about the problems of agricultural development and technology transfer. But only those of the various elites requested that they remain anonymous in this book.

Some of my findings are not rigorously supported by extensive data. And often enough, as in the two chapters on Colombia, certain issues simply defy quantification. There is no way I can put mathematics behind my trust in the small farmer of Colombia. I talked to many of them. They seemed honest people. Besides, what they said simply mirrored the abject poverty I saw all around me. I went to Colombia to see and learn. I went to Colombia because Colombia with all its idiosyncrasies is still a typical underdeveloped country. I did not go there just to fill the gaps in something I had already constructed. What I say about Colombia is uncomfortable to read. It lacks a lot of statistics. Its recommendations are designed to match the needs of the Colombian society in the twenty-first century rather than those of the immediate tomorrow. My view of the need for social reform in Colombia is not exactly a view held by me alone. In a letter dated July 20, 1975, the recently "retired" Colombian Army commander-in-chief, General Alvaro Valencia, wrote that:

> In any country afflicted by "objective conditions" favoring armed revolution, guerillas taking advantage of extremely adequate geographical environment cannot be destroyed by force alone. Social and economic change in the way of roads, agrarian betterment, health service, medical assistance, education, organized transport, are more suitable tools for strategic victory than costly and bloody armed efforts. Perhaps the latter could yield some measure of tactical success but will never uproot a sickness which lies in the depth of an unbalanced society.[35]

Chapters Three and Four of this book are the result of a personal analysis of the Colombian predicament with technology, rural poverty, and rural violence. They make neither comfortable nor pleasant reading. They are somber thinking based on the very unpleasant confrontation with gross inequalities, malnutrition, and extreme rural poverty. They shatter all illusions created by technological developments divorced from their social context. The Colombian rural poor are but a tiny fraction of some 1000 million small subsistence farmers in the low-income regions of the world. The Somalian, the Guatemalan, the Bangladesh, and the Colombian peasants are united by the crushing problems of poverty in their impoverished lands. In El Salvador hundreds of thousands of peasants live in mud huts. Over ninety percent of their children suffer from malnutrition. The poor peasants of El Salvador and those of the other underdeveloped countries are victims of debilitating diseases. In short, what I say about Colombia does transcend the Colombian environment. Poverty has no borders. And rural poverty is timeless. But as these pages will suggest, unless the underdeveloped country elites use technology and social reform to eliminate the threat of breakdown and starvation in the countryside their peasant majorities will become time bombs.

IS HUNGER THE RESULT OF POVERTY?

In 1973 the U.S. government paid over $3 billion to the American farmers for not growing as much food as they could. A year later this policy was abandoned with the result that about 50 million unproductive acres were returned to productive use. Meanwhile, in the Sahel region of Africa where as many as ten million people may still be facing starvation, some of the best land and water resources are not producing food for the 50 million Africans of the area just south of the Sahara. They have instead been put at the disposal of various agribusiness corporations to produce goods for the markets of the rich countries. Latin America, with an area much larger than that of the United States and with a population of only 265 million, imports most of its food. Moreover, 60 percent of that arable land remains fallow at a time when millions of Latin Americans live at levels of extreme poverty. It is these millions of poor, indigent and despondent, who have large families. What, then, is the relationship between food and population? Is hunger the result of rapid population growth, of scarcity, or of plunder? Is the recent world food crisis a manifestation of social injustice in the underdeveloped countries? Before World War II the underdeveloped countries had enough food for their own people. Why have they since become net importers of cereals? What are the reasons for the failure of agriculture in the poor countries to provide adequate supplies of food for local consumption? Do the small farmer and appropriate technologies hold the key to a balanced and sustained growth of the food economies of the underdeveloped countries? The effort of the West to make the big landowner the main food provider of the underdeveloped countries has clearly failed. Are there any alternatives to that strategy?

The purpose of this book is to probe, not to prove. It seeks not answers but the generation of relevant thought and questions that can perhaps help us understand the nature of the human condition defined as it is by the predicament of hunger and poverty. The questions raised above have been raised by countless generations of men. They are as old as human history. That we call our age modern is simply a convenience. To an eighteenth century man his was the modern age. Complexity might have changed in time but the problems of new knowledge, its transfer to a new environment, its adaptability, acceptance, impact on and relation to poverty have remained timeless. For instance, at the turn of the eighteenth century India and France were largely subsistence economies. They had no population or food problem. India in fact exported food. But they both had a poverty problem. From 1720 to 1800 French population rose from about 20 to 27 million people. The French Revolution found the country with about nine million people sunk into poverty. Who were these poor? How did French society treat them? And what did these poor and indigent do to cope with their predicament?

The eighteenth century French poor do not differ much from the poor people of twentieth century India. They lived in the mountain regions and the flatlands. Some were small landowners, some were sharecroppers, and some worked in the rich farmland of the rural elite. Hard times always diminished the thin line that separated the poor from the indigent. The margin of survival for both was narrow. The birth of an extra child meant the certain collapse of the precarious family economy of the poor. Unwanted children were thus abandoned at the doorsteps of the local or city hospitals with minimum chance of survival either because epidemics were raging or because of the lethal environment of the children abandonment centers. The poor coped with their predicament in thousands of ingenious ways. They maintained their makeshift economy through odd jobs, migration, violence, and the stability of their family structure. And when in Paris the price of bread reached the highest point in almost half a century, the poor stormed and destroyed the Bastille. During the French Revolution the poor also managed to undermine some of the legal and institutional foundations of indigence. They destroyed the taxation system and eliminated the hated tithes and seigneurial dues. They also managed to purchase nationalized church land. And in time the French poor learned to limit their number. It took France almost down to the middle of the nineteenth century to avoid the threat posed by the fact that half of its population was on the verge of pauperization. A century later France had a ratio of arable land to population not very different from that of India. And yet today India is importing food while France has considerable surpluses for export.

Chapter One will to some degree trace the roots of backwardness in India. But at this juncture suffice it to say that there is no economic reason to prevent India from repeating the agricultural experience of France, since both countries have an equivalent ratio of arable land to population. Not only do famines hit India in biblical cycles, but agriculture in India still depends on the monsoons. There are few regions in India that provide controlled water supplies for agriculture, and no catchment or water conservation system exists. With very little advanced technology, and a land reform structure that failed on a sustained basis, India will continue to be the victim of famines and of attending dooms of social collapse. Good year harvests do not suffice to provide for the following lean years because of the shocking neglect with which the reserves are stored. To say to the Indian masses that cows can be eaten is to invite lynching. Meanwhile the population in India is increasing at a rate that is inversely proportional to the sufficiency of food. By the year 2000 India will have more than a billion people.

It is a fact that poverty, both in its intellectual and material dimensions, is the root of unbalanced population growth and of backward food production. And these pages will document that the world food problem is above all a poverty problem. Like malnutrition it mirrors and is a manifestation of social injustice. Yet the extent of our understanding and recognition of this global predicament is woefully inadequate, perhaps because we choose to view the world food problem with the intellectual and scientific constraints of the West. Very simply, these constraints make the world food problem a problem of agricultural productivity. This book rejects this unfounded hypothesis. It further argues that in questions relevant to the agricultural modernization of the poor countries it is not the small peasant farmer who is ignorant but the development professional who assumes that the peasant is ignorant.[36] This study also maintains that Western science and technology are important tools for correcting the food imbalance of the poor countries. Many of these non-Western countries have for over a century been the recipients of Western agricultural science and technology. What happened to that stream of knowledge in its migration and transfer? Did it help non-Western societies increase their food production? This book explores these issues in the light of the development predicament and evolution of the poor countries. At this point it is useful to recall that technological decisions and science and technology transfer involve (1) technical knowledge and (2) human values and social judgments.

Food production can be increased by the intensified cultivation of land using advanced technology adapted to the environmental constraints of the locality. Underutilization of the labor force results in low yields per acre. Labor efficiency alone can raise yields. It can also improve the general conditions of the village community. Technological innovations designed to introduce artificial insemination of livestock, to combat plant diseases, and to develop and disseminate high-yielding seeds will undoubtedly open the road to more and better food and set the foundations for agricultural modernity. But if new technologies exist and are continuously being developed for agricultural change, we know precious little about the traditional farmer—certainly the most crucial factor in the successful transfer of agricultural science and technology. In "the realm of human ecology—the interrelations of the peoples of the poor countries to their natural and social environments—the West has little technology to transfer."[37] It is, then, to these two realms, both ecological and technological, that the following pages will address themselves.

The urgency of the world food and poverty problems have led to policy priorities and development strategies that in no way reflect humanity's collective memory on these critical concerns that are as old as human history. To divorce science from its social context is to solve the wrong, if temporary, problem. History, properly used, provides valuable knowledge and a needed reflective perspective in the often complex problems confronting mankind. Historical experience tempers arrogance with wisdom. Facts count in history but so do ideas and values. And the food and poverty question, involving as it does science, the sacred, and the profane, can be treated in isolation from its immensely rich human dimensions only with great injury to objectivity. This study explores those dimensions. The guiding spirit of this study is the belief in the interrelatedness of human problems and knowledge. By its structure of analysis and questions that it raises, this book seeks to elaborate knowledge for effective agricultural development policy. National development is a multiple-dimensional process. And science transfer for agricultural modernization is but one dimension in this human contest for betterment—to improve the quality of life and serve the most urgent needs of the people. But this study also poses a challenge of profound significance in that it seeks practical and ethical criteria for a better future. It will recommend action programs of science and technology transfer for agricultural modernization. In this way it has the possibility to extend technological culture beyond its traditional boundaries. Philosophically, this work transcends the present into a future that is free from fragmenting ideologies and recognizes the global community as the legitimate depository of human needs. Moreover, the conception of the future here is in terms of nontechnological values. This allows for the technique to remain a technique and not be transformed into an end by itself.

I did not write this book to support a hypothesis. The conclusion emerged from the empirical data presented in the text and from my personal confrontation with the brutal realities of backwardness. The origins of this study are not likely to be found in thirst for esoteric research or a desire to open a dialogue with the elite of development specialists. Rather, the genesis and evolution of this essay are related to the need for relevant thought as a basis of understanding of the present world food problem. The specter of famine has had a very long history. But what makes the present food crisis a turning point in the survival of civilized societies is the unprecedented magnitude of global disaster that the world food problem represents. The question here is not merely that two-thirds of mankind do not have enough to eat but that the one-third that eats well seems to be on the verge of abdicating its responsibility to so vast a human tragedy. Writing in 1967, an observer of the Indian phase of this global tragedy said:

> We must permit this man, and millions like him, to sit in some small corner of our consciences. He dies, a victim of the grinding calculus of India's history which adds, unwittingly, too many like himself to a land of minuses. We, the affluent, have not done this to him with cold intent.

It is simply that none of us has really done enough. We have given, with glad trumpeting—of our surpluses. We proudly announce, from our fortress of abundance, a War on Poverty and massive aid to the world's distressed with seven-tenths of one percent of our very gross national product. To self-applause we have settled for less, for minor skirmishes, for painless doles of calculated aid. . . . Stripped of all defense, this man asked for life; a prior right. We surround our fears and riches with higher walls of steel, which serve to mute the melancholy cries of hungry men like this who haunt the world today pleading only for tomorrow's bread, or at very minimum—for the crumbs of our compassion. He dies. And we, behind our billion-dollar parapets, value inverted, find ourselves among the vanquished, our better selves betrayed. Somehow, slow-choked in shiny armament, we have died with him.[38]

Chapter 1

Europe and the Non-Western World: Global Colonization and the Export of Agricultural Technologies

BRINGING CIVILIZATION TO BARBARIAN AND PRIMITIVE PEOPLES

In 1494 the Portuguese and the Spaniards received the blessings of Pope Alexander VI in their formal agreement that divided the world between them. Spain received North and South America. Portugal inherited Africa, India, the Spice Islands and, later, Brazil. Soon the English, Dutch, and French joined this European crusade to colonize the world. With the decline of the Iberian peninsula in the seventeenth and eighteenth centuries the French, Dutch, and English were the main beneficiaries of the Spanish and Portuguese empires outside the Americas. At the end of the eighteenth century Western Europe controlled the ocean routes, with the result that a handful of Europeans developed a huge trade, amassing vast fortunes and profits. This wealth made Europe the only source for global change. And change she did bring in the form of global colonization.

European empire building was based on the pretext of bringing civilization to barbarian and primitive peoples. The Belgian King Leopold told the delegates to the Brussels Geographical Conference of September 1876 that European civilization was guided by a moral, Christian imperative in its efforts to enlighten the less fortunate of the world: "To open up to civilization the sole portion of the globe to which it has not yet penetrated, to pierce the darkness which still envelops whole populations, is, I venture to say, a crusade worthy of this century

25

of progress."[1] The European vanguard of colonialism was made of explorers, hunters, and missionaries. These fortune seekers managed to extract huge concessions from native chiefs or kings. A partner of the great English financier and imperialist Cecil Rhodes (1853–1902) convinced an African king to allow him to exploit the mineral wealth of Southern Rhodesia. In 1889 Rhodes received a royal charter from England that authorized his British South Africa Company to:

> carry into effect divers concessions and agreements which have been made by certain of the chiefs and tribes inhabiting the said region, and such other concessions, agreements, grants, and treaties as they may hereafter obtain within the said region or elsewhere in Africa, with the view to promoting trade, commerce, civilization, and good government. . . .[2]

What kind of people did Rhodes want to civilize? The former governor of Kenya, Phillip Mitchell, described the tribal societies of East and Central Africa as they existed at the turn of the twentieth century:

> Inland of the narrow coastal strip they had no units of government of any size or stability; indeed, with a few exceptions such as Buganda, nothing beyond local chiefs or patriarchs. They had no wheeled transport and, apart from the camels and donkeys of the pastoral nomads, no animal transport either; they had no roads nor towns; no tools except small hand hoes, axes, wooden digging sticks, and the like; no manufactures and no commerce as we understand it, and no currency, although in some places barter of produce was facilitated by the use of small shells; they had never heard of working for wages. They went stark naked or clad in the bark of trees or the skins of animals, and they had no means of writing, even by hieroglyphics, notches on a stick or knots in a piece of grass or fibre; they had no weights and measures of general use. . . . They were pagan spirit or ancestor proprietors, in the grip of magic or witchcraft, their minds cribbed and confined by superstition.[3]

In 1938 the prime minister of Southern Rhodesia explained what happened to the black African thanks to his enforced diet in European civilization:

> Because of the presence of the white man the Bantu is, with accelerating speed, lifting himself out of his primitive conditions. His inter-tribal wars have been prohibited, and his once frequently-recurring epidemics have been checked. His numbers are increasing. Tribes once separated by traditional animosities are developing the idea of racial unity. . . . The Bantu is resolved to learn, and within as yet undetermined limits is capable of learning. To forbid him opportunities is contrary to natural justice, but are we to allow him to develop and in the course of time,

because his requirements are so small, to oust the European? . . . While there is yet time and space, the country should be divided into separate areas for black and white. In the Native area the black man must be allowed to rise to any position to which he is capable of climbing. Every step in the industrial and social pyramid must be open to him, excepting only—and always—the very top. . . . The Native may be his own lawyer, doctor, builder, journalist or priest, and he must be protected from white competition in his own area. In the European area the black man will be welcomed when, tempted by wages, he offers his services as a labourer, but it will be on the understanding that there he shall merely assist, and not compete with, the white man.[4]

The Europeans did not merely brutalize the native. They threatened his very existence. The civilized Europeans avenged the early barbarian invasions of their homelands by killing most of the Indians of both North and South America. The conquest of black Africa and the Spanish colonization of Mexico and Peru were ephemeral if for no other reason than that these non-European peoples were too many to be easily annihilated by the small number of foreign conquerors. In Argentina that memory of barbarism is very much alive today:

There is as yet in Argentina no myth of the noble Indian. The memory of the genocide is too close; it is still something to be dismissed in a line or two in the annals. In Argentina the detestation of the vanished pampa Indian is instinctive and total: the Argentine terror is that people in other countries might think of Argentina as an Indian country.[5]

Europe's grip on the non-Western world was crushing. The Hungarian Orientalist and traveler Arminius Vambery, writing from firsthand observation in the early twentieth century, recorded the global dominance of Europe:

When, comfortably seated in our well-upholstered railway-carriage, we gaze upon the Hyrkanian Steppe, upon the terrible deserts of Karakum and Kisikum, we can scarcely realise the terrors, the sufferings, and the privations, to which travellers formerly were exposed . . . . And great changes similar to those which have taken place in Central Asia may also be noticed in greater or less degree in other parts and regions of the Eastern world: Siberia, West and North China, Mongolia, Manchuria, and Japan were in the first half of the nineteenth century scarcely known to us, and . . . we now find that the supreme power of the Western world is gradually making itself felt. The walls of seclusion are ruthlessly pulled down, and the resistance caused by the favoured superstitions, prejudices, and the ignorance or the sleepy and apathetic man in the East, is slowly being overcome . . . present-day Europe, in its restless, bustling activity will take good care not to let the East relapse again into its former indolence. We forcibly tear its eyes open; we push, jolt, toss, and shake it, and we compel it to exchange its world-worn, hereditary ideas and customs for our modern views of life; nay, we have even succeeded to some extent in convincing our Eastern neighbours, that our civilisation, our faith, our customs, our philosophy, are the only means whereby the well-being, the progress, and the happiness, of the human race can be secured. For well-nigh 300 years we have been carrying on this struggle with the Eastern world, and persist in our unsolicited interference, following in the wake of ancient Rome, which began the work with marked perseverance, but naturally never met with much success because of the inadequate means at its disposal . . . . We may admire the splendor, the might, and the glory of ancient Rome, we may allow that the glitter of its arms struck terror and alarm into the furthest corners of Asia; but in spite of all that, it would be difficult to admit that the civilising influence of Rome was ever more than an external varnish, a transitory glamour. Compared with the real earnest work done in our days by Western Powers, the efforts of Rome are as the flickering of an oil-lamp in comparison with the radiance of the sun in its full glory. It may be said without exaggeration that never in the world's history has one continent exercised such influence over another as has the Europe of our days over Asia.[6]

EARLY MIGRATION OF EUROPEAN AGRICULTURAL KNOWLEDGE

Despite the seventeenth century scientific revolution, Europe in the early part of the eighteenth century could hardly take pride in its low level of technological knowledge. Some of that knowledge had been transferred to Europe from the East. European agriculture surpassed Chinese agriculture in technology only in the nineteenth century. However, the European advances in the exact sciences and the ability of the Europeans to put all that knowledge to practical use led Europe to develop a scientific and technological civilization which sought to transform the world. The accumulated knowledge of this civilization holds the key to material prosperity, and for the current two-thirds of hungry humanity it holds the key to their survival. This is how an educated Christian Arab described why non-Westerners found the scientific and technological achievements of the West so powerful and irresistible:

> Among the factors that wrought for the apotheosis of the West in Eastern minds, the mechanical aspect of European civilization—inventions and scientific appliances—was beyond doubt the most potent. For there was not and never had been anything corresponding to it in the East. Oriental genius had produced great religions, achieved great triumphs in art

and literature, constructed colossal empires, but it had never tamed and canned the elements, packed scientific principles into little mechanical parcels. And it happened that while the intellect of awaking Europe was ferreting out and applying the secrets of nature, the East was passing through a phase of decline and somnolence. When therefore this flood of mechanical inventions burst in upon the Near East towards the end of the 19th and the beginning of the 20th century, Easterners were completely dazzled and fascinated by these undreamt-of wonders and the mysterious power that lay behind them.[7]

The Europeans put a high priority on using the earth. Their migration to the New World started the modern phase of the transfer of agricultural science and technology to non-European peoples. This transfer usually meant the blending of the old with the new. The Europeans who settled North America had no choice but to accept the indigenous corn as a valuable crop. For several years intense cultivation made no sense in America where there was an abundance of rich, virgin land. The American prairies helped the newcomers to start the innovation of summer fallow and dry farming for wheat cultivation. At the same time agricultural tools, implements, and machinery were transferred and even improved overseas. Next to the diffusion in the Americas of Europe's crops, animals, and practices, the transfer of European scientific methods of agriculture in the New World was decisive in food production and agricultural modernization. The practical use of the new knowledge on artificial fertilizers, from bone dust to the fixation of atmospheric nitrogen, revolutionized agricultural production. European advances in genetics also led to improvements in plant and animal breeding. But the countries that benefited from the technology developed by Europe were in the temperate zone, had access to capital, did not have exploding populations, and had themselves developed a diversified technological civilization as the basis of their culture. Besides, these North American nations that absorbed the late eighteenth and nineteenth century technology dealt mainly with a low capital-intensive and simple technology.

The transfer of agricultural science and technology from Europe to other countries was facilitated and institutionalized by the various research centers, experimental farms and stations, botanical gardens, laboratories, and departments of agriculture serving Europe and the European settlers in other regions of the world. This flow of knowledge paid high dividends. The Canadians developed new varieties of wheat, oats and barley. Australia in the early 1900s produced a strain of wheat with rust-resistant qualities. New Zealand contributed to the cultivation of clover and grasses with high feeding value. In the tropics it was the Christian missionaries who imported European agricultural methods. But real advances in tropical agriculture were made in Europe or by Europeans working in the tropics. For instance, Dutch agricultural scientists working in what used to be the Netherland Indies (Indonesia) made pioneering research in plant pathology and soil chemistry.[8] Like most of the institutions transferred to the poor countries in the colonial period, technology was a static instrument designed to perform certain limited functions. It is not that derivative technology cannot give birth to an entrepreneurial activity, but in the imperial system the potential for technological self-renewal was stunted by the lack of competition and by the unchanging technology itself. Industry suffered most severely from this model of development. But because agricultural technology is ecology-specific, it was transferred with care. It was under the colonial rule that tropical agriculture was modernized. European imperial research improved many indigenous crops, domesticated others, and, in general, made agricultural production profitable and plentiful. Continuous research gave a dynamic element to the transfer of agricultural technology: it made it self-renewing. However, this technology was never directed to modernize traditional agriculture. Its singular function was to perfect the production of cash crops—coffee, cocoa, sugar cane, palm nuts, rubber, and peanuts. The legacy of this policy is very much alive today in Africa.

SOCIAL FOUNDATIONS OF AFRICAN AGRICULTURE

In the tribal society and economy of Africa, agriculture evolved into a simple, noncommercial social institution whose sole purpose was to provide enough food for local consumption. With a plentiful supply of land, the Africans used a field for as long as it was fertile and then they abandoned it to move to a new area to cultivate their crops or to graze their livestock. A 1924 document described the agricultural methods of some Africans in Southern Rhodesia in this way:

> It cannot be said that the native of Mashonaland is a good agriculturist; his methods are wasteful and in a way ruinous to the future interests of the country. As a rule bush country is selected for gardens, generally in the granite formation where the soil is easy to dig and cultivate. The trees and shrubs are cut down, the stumps of the trees are left standing three to four feet high in the ground, and in the case of very large trees only the top branches are lopped off. The trunks and branches of the felled trees and brushwood and weeds are gathered in heaps around the stumps. The ground is ridged up in ridges about eighteen inches broad, the portion of ground underneath the ridge is not touched with the hoe,

the soil from the furrows on either side being placed on top of the ridge. The larger trees are not usually lopped until the ground has been dug. Just before the first rains of the season the brushwood around the stumps is burned and dug into the ground. With the first rains a crop of millet and maize is sown, with pumpkins and gourds around the tree stumps. Ground nuts and beans usually have a garden to themselves, with a few mealies [maize] between the rows. On virgin soil a fairly good crop may be expected the first year, but after three years the land is exhausted, and the native cultivator looks for pastures new. No attempt is made to manure the ground, except with the wood ash and weeds which are dug in. It takes about ten to fifteen years for gardens which have been abandoned to recover and be again fit for cultivation.[9]

With the digging stick, the hoe, and the axe as his agricultural implements and without the knowledge or use of manure, selection of seeds, straight line planting, or crop rotation, the African farmer's shifting cultivation made sense. It permitted a sparse population to maintain an ecological balance with its environment. Moreover, African agriculture was structured to serve the tribal community. In this context private ownership of land was forbidden since the land belonged to the community. The individual member of a tribe had the right to cultivate a plot of the communal land sufficient for his needs. In this subsistence agriculture African tribesmen did

> not own land as individuals; it had not occurred to them that land was something that could be owned as a spear was owned; it was something of which a man might have the use if the king agreed, but the right to use it was not something that could be exchanged for something else. It was the king's duty to see that his people were fed and so he gave them land; it was his duty to make the rain; but land was hardly more subject to ownership than rain.[10]

The case of British Uganda illustrates the role of the traditional African farmer in his own subsistence agriculture and in the market agriculture introduced by the British rulers in that African country. Uganda came under English colonial government in the late nineteenth century. This country is in the heart of Africa. It lies within the basin of the upper Nile and the lesser basin of Lake Victoria where climate favors agriculture. The rainfall is reliable and seasonably distributed. The soil is good, enriched as it is with an excellent supply of plant nutrients. There are certain regions in Uganda where perennial crops can be cultivated most successfully. In short, agriculture in Uganda is secure and productive.

The colonial government transferred agricultural science and technology to Uganda but not for bettering subsistence agriculture.

The purpose of the British was to improve the quality of the exported cotton. They also introduced and widely disseminated "that unpalatable and unnutritious but drought-resistant root, cassava." The plow was transferred to Uganda and so was crop rotation. Both innovations failed because they disrupted the soil structure of Uganda.[11] Nevertheless the colonial government grafted specialized forms of production on Uganda's subsistence economy. This was accomplished at a great cost both to human and material resources. And increased wealth meant the impairment of the social structure of the tribal society of this East African country. After war, famine, and pestilence receded, the population of Uganda increased in parallel to the rapid growth in cultivation and production for export. The time was reached when economic development could not be sustained without a radical reorganization of Uganda's social structure:

> By 1930 the people of Uganda had settled down to the new way of life that had been mapped out for them by British rule and the railway. It was a quiet, on the whole an unexciting and unexacting life. There was no more war and no more politics except in a very muted form. Person and property were as secure as laws and magistrates could make them. The impact of external trade had been absorbed and the economy reconstituted on a new basis, of which the essential element was the production of cotton, supplemented by the production of coffee in Bugisu and parts of Buganda, of tobacco in Bunyoro and of groundnuts in the Eastern and Northern Provinces. The effect of economic change on the lives of the people had, on the whole, been surprisingly small, whether it is the pattern of activity or the pattern of consumption that is brought under review. They had not to any considerable extent been either driven or drawn into systems of production that were fundamentally novel in organisation or technique. They did not figure at all in the higher echelons of enterprise, which were manned exclusively by members of the immigrant communities. They took no part in the export-import trade, or, except as labourers, in the processing of crops; even in retail commerce they were eclipsed by Asian traders; they had produced no members of the liberal professions, other than teachers and clergy, and very few highly skilled workers. It was only in agricultural production that Africans could really be said to contribute largely to the functioning of the exchange economy. In this sphere the change had indeed been a thorough-going one. It was now accepted that the cultivation of the soil, that is, the production of seed-cotton, was the normal and proper occupation for the great majority of men, and this implied a revolutionary change in the mode of life of men belonging to the "planting" tribes, though less so for the seed-farmers. The cotton plot had become almost as integral, by now almost as traditional-seeming, a part of the standard peasant holdings as the banana grove or the millet field. Production for

the overseas market had been grafted on the subsistence farming, and with very little disturbance of the parent stock. In Buganda and Busoga the cotton field took its place beside the banana grove, along with the beans and sweet potatoes and other seasonal crops which had always figured in the agricultural system. In the drier areas further north and east cotton was woven into the customary rough-and-ready crop rotation, being normally planted after the harvesting of the main crop of finger-millet. An acre or two was thus added to the cultivated area of each homestead, but, except on a few estates in Buganda, the general scale of farming operations had not been sensibly altered. Nor—and here the big cotton-farmers of Buganda were no exception—had the techniques. Virtually the only technical innovation had been the substitution of imported steel hoes for the local iron product. Ploughing had made a certain headway, but only in limited areas of the Eastern Province.[12]

Under the European imperial rule the transfer of agricultural science and technology to the non-Western world was limited and specifically designed to increase the yields of cash crops. Colonialism exploited native resources often for the benefit of private investors and consumers.[13] The imperial rule impoverished the colonial village.[14]

COLONIALISM AND THE IMPOVERISHMENT OF THE VILLAGE IN INDIA

India became a classic model in modern colonial society and economy coming face to face with European civilization in the eighteenth century when it was conquered by England. With a complex structure of diverse traditions, with Hinduism's tolerance for other religions, and with deeply divided social classes, India was unable to withstand Western influence flowing through the English colonial order. The British constructed India's railways. They provided the banking and insurance facilities for an expanding economy and spread Western ideas and technology on health, education, and economic life. In short, India's interests and capabilities were directed to serve first and foremost those of England. The Indian village and its social structure paid a dear price to the English master. The village in India was a self-sufficient agrarian community whose economic activities were for the most part noncommercial. The Indian farmer cultivated his share of the village land and paid his tax in kind to the government. Ancient tradition and religion and a fixed relationship in terms of services, duties, and responsibilities were the forces that made the village society a very intimate and secure one. Moreover, in this social agrarian structure it was not the individual who mattered but the joint family and the caste. All this was disrupted with the coming of British rule. The British East India Company that governed India for almost two centuries started to tax the Indian peasant. To maximize its revenues, the company introduced a new land tenure system that essentially made the tax collectors into English style landlords. This policy made the Indian peasant a tenant. It forced him off his land since he could rarely pay a fixed cash land tax. Land could be bought, sold, mortgaged, and lost. Entire villages belonged to individual proprietors or to landlords.[15] The English destroyed the Indian village and with it they almost made possible the continuous breakdown of Indian society. Furthermore, the English masters not only did not encourage manufacturing in India but they took active steps to discourage it. Their high import duty to Indian cotton goods dealt a severe blow to a flourishing industry and displaced millions of spinners, weavers, and other artisans. The cotton fabrics of India were of "extraordinary perfection" and had for centuries dominated the world's markets:

> The Indians have in all ages maintained an unapproached and almost incredible perfection in their fabrics of cotton. Some of their muslins might be thought the work of fairies, or of insects, rather than of men; but these are produced in small quantities, and have seldom been exported. In the same province from which the ancient Greeks obtained the fine muslins then known, namely, the province of Bengal, these astonishing fabrics are manufactured to the present day.[16]

INDIAN AGRICULTURE IN THE EIGHTEENTH CENTURY

After serving the British empire in India for thirty years, the English General Alexander Walker (1764–1831) wrote a brief essay on Indian agriculture that remained unpublished for a century and a half. From this essay Walker appears to have been a man of broad erudition. With a rare sensitivity to the Indian traditions and a keen eye for scientific observation, Walker's account of eighteenth century Indian agriculture is a valuable, objective source on both the social and scientific context of India agrarian life and experience. It helps us look at the present food problem of India with scientific detachment. It also helps us understand that India has both the scientific and the human potential for agricultural modernization. Agricultural science and technology transfer to India has a long tradition. Walker's essay will be quoted here rather extensively:

> In Malabar the knowledge of Husbandry seems as ancient as their History. It is the favourite employment of the inhabitants. It is endeared

to them by their mode of life, and the property which they possess in the soil. It is a theme for their writers; it is a subject on which they delight to converse, and with which all ranks profess to be acquainted. They have provided a code of rules for good husbandry. A system is laid down for the proper cultivation of the soil. The rights of the proprietor and of the mere occupier of land are distinguished and explained. The Husbandman is protected. The proprietor is secured against bad management, while the cultivator or improver is encouraged . . . . Nothing should surprise us more in the present condition of the Indian cultivator than his persevering industry, and well cultivated fields. Any other than a people of a very buoyant spirit would have sunk under these circumstances.

The Hindoos have been long in possession of one of the most beautiful and useful inventions in agriculture. This is the Drill Plough. This instrument has been in use from the remotest times in India. I never however observed it in Malabar, as it is not required in rice cultivation in which its advantages have been superceded by transplanting. The system of transplanting is only in fact another method of obtaining the same object as by Drill Husbandry. It would be but just to adduce this, as another proof of the ingenuity of this people and of their successful attention to this branch of labour. They have different kinds of ploughs, both Drill and common, adapted to different sorts of seed, and soils.

They have a variety of implements for husbandry purposes, some of which have only been introduced into England in the course of our recent improvements. They clean their fields both by hoeing and weeding; they have weeding ploughs, which root out and extirpate the weeds. A roller would be useless on rice grounds, which are always wet, and frequently an equal mixture of water and mud. The place of the roller is supplied by an instrument which levels or smooths the ground, without turning on an axis. They have also Mallets for breaking clods, the usual assortment of Hoes, Harrows and Rakes.

It has been objected to these instruments that they are simple, clumsy and rude. This does not however make them less useful. Simplicity cannot surely be counted a fault; in some of our districts the plough is by far too complicated a machine. They are not unhandy to the people who have been in the habit of using them. They appear awkward to us because we have not been in that habit, and because the Indian Husbandman can afford to throw away nothing on ornament. The same instrument painted and smoothed by the plane would have given a very different idea of its value. The judgment of the eye decides more than we imagine. All this however depends rather upon taste and opulence, than on utility. The circumstances of an Indian Husbandman are not to be compared to those of our substantial tenants. They can study effect and appearance, which are in fact essential to their credit as good farmers. It is not however very long since we have painted and polished our ploughs. I have seen them within these few years in some parts of the country covered by the unremoved bark of the tree.

The numerous ploughings of the Hindoo Husbandman have been urged as a proof of the imperfection of his instrument; but in reality they are a proof of the perfection of his art. It is not only to extirpate weeds that the Indian Husbandman re-ploughs and cross-ploughs; it is also to loosen the soil, apt to become hard and dry under a tropical sun; and hence it becomes necessary to open the earth for air, dew and rain. These advantages can only be obtained by exposing a new surface from time to time to the atmosphere. In India dews fall much more copiously than they do with us, and they are powerful agents in fertilising land. Weeds also increase with a quickness, and a luxuriance, of which we can form but an imperfect idea in this country. These are sufficient causes for the frequent operation of ploughing, without the necessity of blaming either the Husbandman or his implement. The frequency of ploughing must depend everywhere on the nature of the soil, its situation, and the purpose for which it is intended. In some cases, our farmers in this country, plough three or four, and even as often as six times.

It is the practice in many parts of India, to sow different species of seeds in the same field. This practice has been censured, but it is probably done for the same reason that our farmers sow rye-grass and clover with wheat, barley, or oats; tares with rye; beans and peas; vetches and corn, etc.

It has been found by experience that these crops not only thrive in the same field; but improve each other. Rye and oats for instance, serve to support the weak creeping tares, and add besides to the bulk of the crop by growing through the interstices. Clover and rye grass are sheltered by the corn. This analogy will apply to the Husbandry of India. These similar experiments may be carried further, where the climate and soil are superior. In India different kinds of seeds when sown in the same field are kept separate by the Drill, or they are mixed together, and sown broadcast. In the last case they are commonly cut down as forage. A plant called sota gowar, is sown broadcast with sugar cane, in Guzerat. The gowar serves as a shelter to the sugar cane, from the violent heat of the sun, during the most scorching season of the year. Joar and badgery are sown together, in the same country late, not for the sake of a crop, but for straw, which is very nutritive, and very abundant. This is one of the instances in which the natives provide a green crop for their cattle. Other grains are sown both together and separately, merely for their straw . . . .

It is evident that these examples are not founded on bad principles, and that they are in conformity with the best practice of farming. They evince the care of the Hindoo Husbandman to provide food for his labouring cattle . . . . In many parts of India the fields are fenced and enclosed. This is the case wherever the people live in quiet and security. It is sufficient to show what was the ancient practice, when the Government was good and the country not exposed to the ravages of war. In Guzerat this attention to the security of property was seldom neglected. Even during the native Government, the Ryot was protected in his revenue engagements; in case he might not be able to fulfill them, either from war or adverse seasons. This was effected, by exempting him in his lease, on the event of any of these circumstances occurring, by the phrase 'Asmani Sultanee'. The enclosures are generally of a square form. The divisions are seldom very large, and are of unequal sizes according to the judgment, interest, or taste of the proprietor. They are remarkably neat, kept clean, and well dressed. These fields have frequently broad grassy margins which are left for pasture, such as are seen in some parts of Yorkshire. The whole world does not produce finer and more beautifully cultivated fields than those in Guzerat . . . .

I have seen from Cape Comorin to the Gulph of Kutch details of the most laborious cultivation, of the collection of manure, of grain sown for fodder, of grain sown promiscuously for the same purpose; of an attention to the change of seed, of fallows, and rotation of crops. The rotation may sometimes be imperfectly followed; but it is a system understood and acted upon throughout India, with more or less skill and intelligence . . . .

In every part however that I have visited the application of manure for recruiting and restoring land is well understood. The people seem to have all the resources that we have in this respect. By littering their cattle with straw, they increase the quantity of manure. They collect leaves, and putrescent substances. When they have no means of rotting the straw, they mix it with dry dung, old grass and even branches of trees, which they place in a heap and set fire to it. The ashes are then spread on the ground. The slime and bottoms of tanks are dug up, and considered to be a valuable manure . . . .

The practice of watering and irrigation is not peculiar to the Husbandry of India, but it has probably been carried there to a greater extent, and more laborious ingenuity displayed in it than in any other country. The vast and numerous tanks, reservoirs, and artificial lakes as well as dams of solid masonry in rivers which they constructed for the purpose of fertilizing their fields, show the extreme solicitude which they had to secure this object . . . .

I must repeat that I have seen in India the most abundant crops 'the corn standing as thick on the ground as the land could well bear it'; fields neat, clean and generally without a weed. Infinite pains are taken to extirpate these, and several ingenious instruments have been contrived for the purpose.

It is hardly possible that a weed can be found in a transplanted field, where every stalk is put in by the hand, and carefully planted.

The Husbandman in fine labours incessantly to increase his produce, varying his operations according to circumstances, and acting always when he can, on fixed principles. A system of rotation is attended to, but the alluvial deposits make it in many places unnecessary, and local peculiarities, local oppressions, and the want of resources compels the cultivator to forego many advantages: he is obliged no doubt by so many pressing necessities too often to deviate from the best plan; to submit to such shifts and expedients as are within his power. Some allowance should be made for the circumstances of the people, general as well as particular. Some compassion should be felt for their situation, and when we see one district highly cultivated, another in poverty, and the wrecks everywhere of a greater agricultural prosperity in former times, would it not be equitable and just to conclude that ignorance and stupidity were not the sole causes of these anomalous appearances? The flying surveys, partial, and hasty reports that have as yet only been made of their agriculture, are not to be depended upon. It would require the leisure and application of years, much patience and knowledge of the subject, and a judicious allowance for the peculiarities of the climate, to appreciate either the merits or defects of Hindoo Husbandry. In the present political state of India, the connection and dependence of the greatest part of that fine country on the British Government, renders it an imperious duty for us to use every prudent and proper means for the improvement of its condition; but we should be careful in these attempts at amelioration not to throw it back, and to obstruct its progress, by too hastily condemning the practices of the country, which have been sanctioned by experience, and have their utility in local circumstances. *The minds and inclination of the people should be consulted wherever their own interests are concerned. In general their experience is the best guide.* It is in vain to suggest expensive improvements where there is no capital, where the rent is taken as a tax by Government, and where the proprietory right of the soil is disputed. The cultivation of grain in some places yields no profit to the Husbandman, beyond his mere subsistence. In this case there is neither means, nor stimulus for improvement. Notwithstanding all these disadvantages, the state of agriculture among the Hindoos is respectable: I may say wonderful. Some of the details of their management would furnish information to the European farmer; *when they follow a bad system, it is not from ignorance of the true principles of the art, but from poverty and oppression*; remove these and improvement would follow. The Hindoos, whatever may be their moral qualities, are a temperate and an industrious people, knowing, and well acquainted with their own interests. *In the course of our intercourse with them they have adopted many things from Europe, and they are continually adding when it suits their taste and conveniency. If their system of agriculture is bad, they will alter it as soon as we can show them a cheaper and an easier way of procuring more abundant harvests; but this will not be produced by mere theoretical recommendations. We should succeed in altering many of the habits and practices of India, provided it were possible to compel our own habits to mix with the labours of the people.* (Emphasis mine.)[17]

In the early 1780s the East India Company transferred agricultural technology to a selected group of Indian peasants. Alexander Walker described what happened:

I remember that almost 40 years ago [c. 1780s] an experiment was made on Salsette by delivering to the natives English ploughs and agricultural implements. Some active and enterprising Mahrattah Husbandmen who had but few prejudices were procured: a village was built for them, they were furnished with seed and cattle. They entered on the trial of their own accord and choice. Having adopted the measure it was their interest that it should succeed, and there was no reason that I could ever discover that it failed through any negligence or misconduct of theirs. That it did fail however is certain, and as usual we imputed the failure to the prejudices, sloth, and obstinacy of the natives. I firmly believe however that they judiciously rejected the whole of the cumbrous European machinery. They objected that the plough was too heavy: that the labourer and his oxen were needlessly fatigued: that it therefore performed less work, and that this was not better done for the purpose required than the work of their own plough. It was next observed that the plough was too costly, and similar objections were made to the greatest part of the European equipment. I would not say that this experiment was decisive, or that they have nothing to learn from us, but before we charge them with ignorance and obstinacy for neglecting to adopt our recommendations, we should first be sure of two things; that the new system would give them more abundant harvests, at less expense and labour; and that we have taken all the means and care that were within our power, for their instruction in the art? It should also be well considered how far our agricultural process is suited to the cultivation of rice, the great crop of India, and of which we have no experience.[18]

The Indian peasant saw many invaders. Yet the Indian village community remained relatively unchanged. The English governor of India, Charles Metcalfe, noted in 1830 that:

The village communities are little republics, having nearly every thing they want within themselves, and almost independent of any foreign relations. They seem to last where nothing else lasts. Dynasty after dynasty tumbles down; revolution succeeds to revolution; Hindu, Pathan, Mahratta, Sikh, English, are masters in turn; but the village communities remain the same. In times of trouble they arm and fortify themselves; a hostile army passes through the country; the Village Community collect their cattle within their walls, and let the army pass unprovoked; if plunder and devastation be directed against themselves and the force employed be irresistable, they flee to friendly villages at a distance, but when the storm has passed over they return and resume their occupation. If a country remains for a series of years a scene of continual pillage and massacre, so that the villages cannot be inhabited, the villagers nevertheless return whenever the power of peaceable possession revives. A generation may pass away, but the succeeding generations will return. The sons will take the place of their fathers, the same site for the village, the same position for the houses, the same lands will be reoccupied by the descendants of those who were driven out when the village was depopulated; and it is not a trifling matter that will drive them out, for they will often maintain their posts through times of disturbance and convulsion, and acquire strength to resist pillage and oppression with success.[19]

The pillar of the Indian village community was the peasant. Alexander Walker wrote that:

> The Indian peasant is commonly well enough informed as to his interest, and he is generally intelligent and reflecting. This is the character of his class everywhere. He is attached to his own modes, because they are easy and useful; but furnish him with instruction and means, and he will adopt them, provided they be for his profit. He will not be led away by speculation and theory, which he cannot afford to follow; but he will not refuse any more economical, and less laborious mode of cultivation. He must have prejudices and ancient habits, which it would be difficult to shake; but let him clearly understand that the change would give him less trouble and better crops, and he would adopt it.[20]

The peasant was "the poorest man in India." He was burdened with debts and was the hardest hit by the recurring famines. And yet the colonial government saw fit to tax the Indian peasant even more in order to pay for the irrigation works. The inability of the peasant to meet his tax obligations meant the end of his water supplies. "That was the real cause of failure of irrigations of which the Government complained."[21]

NATURALIZATION OF IMPORTED KNOWLEDGE IN JAPAN

Japan, like India, was forced to open its doors to the West. But unlike India, Japan escaped the crushing grip of colonialism. Japan came in contact with the West in the midsixteenth century. For three more centuries Japan resisted open relations with the Europeans. But when force made Japan vulnerable to European civilization, Japan chose only those European tools that guaranteed material wealth and ability to make war. In the Meiji period (1868–1912) Japan used European science and technology to modernize its industrial and agricultural sectors. Japan assimilated Western technological civilization so fast that in 1894 she defeated China and in 1905 she defeated Russia. That Japan alone of all non-European societies was able to use Western science and technology as a catalyst to modernization indicated that this Asian people had the social and institutional structure for such a transformation. This allowed for a remarkable adaptability of a new knowledge, and its intelligent use at a minimum social cost. The relatively small area of the Japanese islands facilitated the spread of new ideas throughout the country. Japan had a long tradition of borrowing from the Chinese civilization. Her contact with the West in the nineteenth century was a continuation in the trade of ideas. Japan also had a rising merchant class at the critical juncture of the Western impact. She had given the military a top priority in the social structure which inevitably brought into sharp focus Western military technology and made it a valuable commodity to borrow. Moreover, even during her centuries of seclusion Japan permitted Western knowledge to flow into the country. The Dutch were the medium for such a transfer. They were allowed to trade so that they could inform the Japanese of European developments.

Simultaneously, the Japanese studied foreign languages, and in their education the teaching of the physical sciences were both extensive and modern. In the 1790s a Japanese scholar had this to say about Europe:

> When it comes to grand edifices, no country in the world can compare with England. There is no country comparable to England in the manufacture of very fine things. Among the articles which have been imported into Japan by the Dutch, there have been none more precious than the watches. Some of them are so exquisite that hairs are split to make them. London is considered to produce the finest such workmanship in the world. Next comes Paris, in France, and then Amsterdam in Holland. In these three capitals live people virtually without a peer in the world, who are the handsomest of men . . . . Why is it that the people of these three cities, who are human beings like everyone else, have attained such excellence?[22]

At about the same time the emperor of China, Ch'ien lung, informed King George III of England that he had no use for the barbarian West or its technological civilization:

> You, O King, live beyond the confines of many seas, nevertheless, impelled by your humble desire to partake of the benefits of our civilization, you have despatched a mission respectfully bearing your memorial. . . . I have perused your memorial: the earnest terms in which it is couched reveal a respectful humility on your part, which is highly praiseworthy.
>
> In consideration of the fact that your Ambassador and his deputy have come a long way with your memorial and tribute, I have shown them high favour and have allowed them to be introduced into my presence. To manifest my indulgence, I have entertained them at a banquet and made them numerous gifts . . . .
>
> As to your entreaty to send one of your nationals to be accredited to my Celestial Court and to be in control of your country's trade with China,

this request is contrary to all usage of my dynasty and cannot possibly be entertained . . . . If you assert that your reverence for Our Celestial dynasty fills you with a desire to acquire our civilization, our ceremonies and code of laws differ so completely from your own that, even if your Envoy were able to acquire the rudiments of our civilization, you could not possibly transplant our manners and customs to your alien soil. Therefore, however adept the Envoy might become, nothing would be gained thereby.

Swaying the wide world, I have but one aim in view, namely, to maintain a perfect governance and to fulfill the duties of the State: strange and costly objects do not interest me. If I have commanded that the tribute offerings sent by you, O King, are to be accepted, this was solely in consideration for the spirit which prompted you to despatch them from afar. Our dynasty's majestic virtue has penetrated into every country under Heaven, and Kings of all nations have offered their costly tribute by land and sea. As your Ambassador can see for himself, we possess all things. I set no value on objects strange or ingenious, and have no use for your country's manufactures.[23]

Considering the attitude of Japan and China toward the West Lord Elgin prophetically said:

One result of the difference between the habits and the mode of feeling of the Chinese and the Japanese is undoubtedly this, that as the Chinese are steadily retrograding and will in all probability continue to do so until the Empire falls to pieces, the Japanese, if not actually in a state of progressive advancement, are in a condition to profit by the flood of light that is about to be poured into them and to take advantage of these improvements and inventions which the Chinese regard with contemptuous scorn, but which the Japanese will in all probability, when they come to know us better, be both able and anxious to adopt.[24]

The Japanese themselves found it exceedingly difficult to understand why China was unwilling to embark on a program of modernization. Following China's defeat by Japan in 1894 this exchange took place between the Chinese representative for peace negotiations, Li Hung-chang, and the Japanese envoy, Ito Hirobumi:

ITO: Ten years ago when I was at Tientsin, I talked about reform with the grand secretary [Li Hung-chang]. Why is it that up to now not a single thing has been changed or reformed? This I deeply regret.

LI: At that time when I heard you, sir, talking about that, I was overcome with admiration, and furthermore I deeply admired, sir, your having vigorously changed your customs in Japan so as to reach the present stage. Affairs in my country have been so confined by tradition that I could not accomplish what I desired.

ITO: "The providence of heaven has no affection, except for the virtu-
ous." If your honorable country wishes to exert itself to action, Heaven
above would certainly help your honorable country to fulfill its desires. It
is because Heaven treats the people below without discrimination. The
essential thing is that each country should do its own best.[25]

JAPANESE PEASANT CLASS

The Japanese peasant was severely restricted in his social activities.
In 1649 he was ordered to observe, among other things, the following:

> Farm work must be done with the greatest diligence. Planting must be
> neat, all weeds must be removed, and on the borders of both wet and dry
> fields beans or similar foodstuffs are to be grown, however small the
> space.
> Peasants must rise early and cut grass before cultivating the fields. In
> the evening they are to make straw rope or straw bags, all such work to
> be done with great care.
> They must not buy tea or sake to drink, nor must their wives.
> Men must plant bamboo or trees round the farm house and must use
> the fallen leaves for fuel so as to save expense.
> Peasants are people without sense or forethought. Therefore they must
> not give rice to their wives and children at harvest time, but must save
> their food for the future. They should eat millet, vegetables, and other
> coarse food instead of rice. Even the fallen leaves of plants should be
> saved as food against famine . . . . During the seasons of planting and
> harvesting, however, when the labour is arduous the food taken may be a
> little better than usual.
> The husband must work in the fields, the wife must work at the loom.
> Both must do night work. However good-looking a wife may be, if she
> neglects her household duties by drinking tea or sightseeing or rambling
> on the hillsides, she must be divorced.
> Peasants must wear only cotton or hemp—no silk. They may not
> smoke tobacco. It is harmful to health, it takes up time, and costs money.
> It also creates risk of fire.[26]

Not all Japanese peasants owned the land they cultivated. Many were
tenants. And the tenant in Japan was in no way better than the
Russian, Indian, or Europen serf. According to a document issued by a
Japanese landlord in 1725:

> Tenants were not to leave the village on a visit or to put up relatives for
> more than five days without reporting the reasons to the landlord; they
> were strictly forbidden to lodge wandering priests, pilgrims, and other
> strangers even for a single night. They were to avoid ostentation and
> expensive things. . . . They were not to put new roofs on their houses or
> otherwise repair them without the landlord's permission. All "luxurious"

things in their houses . . . were ruled out, but gables, which had been forbidden in the past, were now allowed. They were to show due respect at all times to the landlord and his family and servants and the *hyakusho* [landholder] of the village. They were not to wear footgear in the presence of the landlord, nor to adopt a family insignia resembling his, nor to use a character in a name that was in use in his family, and so on.[27]

The Japanese peasantry was not a static, homogeneous class. Hierarchic and economic disparities were facts of life for the farmers of Japan. An 1816 document permits a look at the peasants who lived like city aristocrats:

> Now the most lamentable abuse (of the present day among the peasants) is that those who have become wealthy forget their status and live luxuriously like city aristocrats. Their houses are as different (from those of the common folk) as day and night or clouds and mud. They build them with the most handsome and wonderful gates, porches, beams, alcoves, ornamental shelves, and libraries . . . . Moreover, village officials and others of wealth entrust cultivation to servants; they themselves wear fine clothes and emulate the ceremonial style of warriors on all such occasions as weddings, celebrations, and masses for the dear . . . . They keep masterless warriors around them and study military arts unsuitable to their status; they take teachers . . . and study the Chinese and Japanese style of writing and painting.[28]

AGRICULTURAL MODERNIZATION IN JAPAN

Only 16 percent of the total land area in Japan is arable. And all of it is cultivated despite the fact that a considerable segment of this very limited resource has thin, acidic, infertile soil. The climate in Japan is no more favorable to agriculture than the soil is. Floods, typhoons, and cold or dry spells cause extensive damage to crops. The English preacher Arthur Hatch visited Japan in 1620. In a letter dated November 25, 1623, he wrote:

> The Countrey of Japan is very lange and spacious, consisting of several Ilands and pettie Provinces; it is Mountainous and craggie, full of Rockes and stonie places, so that the third part of this Empire is not inhabited or manured; neither indeed doth it affoord that occomodation for Inhabitants which is needfull, or that fatnesse and conveniencie for the growth of Corne, Fruit, and small grayne as is requisite; which causeth the people to select the choysest and plainest parts and places of the land both to till and swell in. The Climate is temperate and healthie not much pestred with infectious or obnoxious ayres, but very subject to fierce windes, tempestuous stormes, and terrible Earthquakes, insomuch that both Ships in the harbour have been over-set, and driven ashore by the

furie of the one, and Houses on the land desjoynted and shaken to pieces by the fearefull trembling of the other.[29]

The transfer of agricultural science and technology to Japan before World War I took the form of better irrigation and drainage facilities, superior seeds, improved methods of crop cultivation, and the use of manures and fertilizers. The increased application of fertilizer to new, improved seeds led to a remarkable agricultural productivity. Thanks to innovations in the fertilizer technology, the Japanese farmer had sufficient amounts of fertilizer at low prices.[30] And yet farm mechanization was virtually nonexistent. When it was necessary to reclaim land for paddy rice fields, the landlords or the government put up the needed capital. Incentives existed for this modernization. Landlords received high rent in kind. And the price of rice increased continuously. Absentee owners were not many. Most landowners lived in their rural communities. They encouraged the introduction of innovation especially suited for the needs of the small family farm.[31]

Japanese agricultural growth was realized in the traditional and institutional arrangements of the rural and small family farm. The small family farm averaged about one hectare per household. The land was cultivated by peasant proprietors and tenants. No effort was made to consolidate the widely scattered tiny plots. And there was no rural exodus to the cities. The inherited system of land tenure with its emphasis on the welfare of the small proprietor added to the vitality of the Japanese farming community. Such a rural vitality and stability can perhaps be understood if the strength of the family structure is added to the Japanese respect of farming as a way of life.[32] Rice has been the supreme crop of Jananese agriculture. The farmer in Japan is so much attached to rice that

[h]e pours his and the family's labor into the farm as if it were a matter of love and not of the market. Often, he appears to prefer crops and cultural practices that require more work. He exhibits a strange propensity for exerting more than is economic, and at times, even essential. His yard is usually weedy. But never the fields. Yet, he knows full well that those last blades of grass that he pulls out of his paddy so laboriously do not affect his production by an ounce. Transplanting of rice seedlings is done with similar excessive care. It is neat, precise, and meticulous, like an embroidery on silk.[33]

AGRICULTURE IN INDIA SINCE INDEPENDENCE

Agriculture has been the backbone of India. It provides a livelihood for about 75 percent of the population and contributes about 50 percent of the national income. Moreover, about 50 percent of the country's foreign exchange earnings come from agricultural export sales. These facts indicate that Indian social and economic development depend largely on the future of agricultural modernization.[34] According to Lakshmi Kant Jha, ambassador of India to the United States, the Indian government, since independence in 1947, was aware of the seriousness of the food problem:

> When India attained independence in 1947, memories of the Bengal famine of 1942 were still fresh. The "Grow More Food" campaign, organized in the early postwar years, proved to be the forerunner of the more systematic Community Development and National Extension Services which formed part of the Five Year Plans. Conscious of the fact that the import of food grains consumed vast sums of foreign exchange and aggravated price stability, the government allocated sizable resources to efforts to increase domestic cereal production. The expansion of both major and minor irrigation facilities; the early experiments with improved techniques of cultivation, such as the Japanese method of rice cultivation; the development of the cooperative movement to improve credit as well as marketing facilities; legislative and other measures for the establishment of regulated markets; and a host of other government programs slowly generated the basic infrastructure for rapid agricultural growth. India's foodgrain production rose from 55 million tons to 89 million tons over twenty years. This was followed by a sharp drop in foodgrain production to 72 million tons at the low point of the drought years [midsixties].[35]

Another Indian official, D.V. Reddy, extension commissioner, has also argued that since 1947 India did take steps to transform the social and economic life of the peasant. These steps included land reform and the establishment of institutional structures to educate the Indian peasant in the use and benefits of "improved seeds, chemical fertilizer, insecticides, plant protection equipment, improved agricultural implements and irrigation works." These policies and the Ford Foundation–inspired "package of improved practices and services" helped the peasants to develop "a new and different attitude towards agriculture, towards their neighbors and towards themselves. They are increasingly becoming 'yield-conscious' and 'money-conscious'."[36] India chose "a *planned process* of change" in order to put her scarce resources to optimum use. Neither the laissez-faire nor the "autocratic approach" to agricultural development suited Indian political and economic conditions. Instead, "a progressive democratic approach" to development enabled Indian planners to engage in "a systematic and well-planned effort" to solve their country's food problem.[37] Moreover, according to Reddy, the peasant is at the heart of the Indian agricultural strategy:

Our agricultural strategy, based mainly on an approach of intensive agriculture, has brought into play a number of external stimuli designed to change the behavior of the farmers. Some of the principal stimuli, or, in other words, forces of changes may be indicated as a strengthened extension machinery created at the district and block level, provision of trained and skilled manpower through organisation of systematic and regular training programmes, formulation of specific package of practices for each area, individual farm planning, extension education support through a large net-work of composite type of field demonstrations and wide-spread dissemination of information through an intensive use of the various audio-visual aids, arrangements for adequate supply of production requisites strengthened credit and marketing institutions and, last but not the least, price assurance.[38]

By the midsixties more than 60 million farm households in India cultivated a total of 330 million acres of arable land. But the yields were very low. C. Subramaniam, the then minister of food and agriculture, in an interview dated December 28, 1966, explained the failure of Indian agriculture in these terms:

It is because so far, our effort had been to intensify in the same old traditional way. But simply more intensification of irrigation gives only marginal increase. Or traditional seeds and manures—they do not give a dramatic increase in yields. Our effort so far has been to intensify the traditional methods. But after centuries of cultivation our forefathers had already reached the optimum in the use of traditional methods. So any increase is only marginal. That is why our farmers have not been interested.[39]

Subramaniam's interviewer went to the district of Tanjore where he talked to some Indian peasant farmers. The district of Tanjore in the state of Madras has fertile land. What is more, this land is irrigated, has good rainfall, and has been cultivating rice for centuries. Since 1960 Tanjore benefited from all the programs of the Indian government to increase agricultural production. In this physical context one would expect the farmer to enjoy prosperity and bountiful harvests. But this is not the case for all the farmers of this rich land.

One Tanjore landowner using a wooden plow to cultivate 25 irrigated acres of rice explained why his yield was not what it could have been. It is important to note that this landowner did not do the actual cultivation. He hired daily wage labor to sow, transplant, and harvest. When interviewed in the late sixties he said:

I can't say I am getting the maximum yield. I get around 2000 pounds of rough rice per acre now. I can easily double it. But this is a communist area. There is always labor trouble. They do not work efficiently. Operations get delayed. They are not done on time. Also, drainage is bad. We are desilting only the main channels. But the field channels are not desilted. Under the Act, it has to be done by the cultivator. In case of tenants it should be enforced in some manner. In many cases, landowners also are not doing it.[40]

Other small owner-cultivators admitted that they simply did not use the traditional methods efficiently. "What we do now usually is to throw in some fertilizer when we see the crop looking yellowish." As for the agricultural laborers of Tanjore they followed the orders of the landowners. "He did not ask me to weed this year, so I didn't." And working for wages offered no incentive to the laborer to do a good job.[41]

INDIAN ARITHMETIC OF HUNGER

These simple Indian farmers said more about Indian agriculture and agricultural technology transfer than the meaningless rhetoric of the Indian officials planning agricultural strategies. What the farmers said adds to the Indian arithmetic of hunger. Unlike the Japanese farmer with his small but beloved farm, the Indian small farmer through two centuries of colonial and postcolonial neglect literally does not care what he does with his small plot as long as he produces enough to eat. This does not mean that the Indian peasant is against profits, better methods, technology, and modernization. It has already been shown that such has not been the case. For instance, in a late fifties document we read:

> An observer in [the village of] Senapur [in North Central India] cannot help but be impressed with the way the village uses its physical resources. The age-old techniques have been refined and sharpened by countless years of experience, and each generation seems to have had its experimenters who added a bit here and changed a practice there, and thus improved the community lore. Rotations, tillage and cultivation practices, seed rates, irrigation techniques, and the ability of the blacksmith and potter to work under handicaps of little power and inferior materials, all attest to a cultural heritage that is richly endowed with empirical wisdom.[42]

The indifference of the Indian peasant, his apparent inability to produce as much as he could, must rather be seen as a symptom of a general technological disease afflicting Indian policy and polity since 1947. Japan used her surpluses from agriculture to finance her industrialization.[43] In the period from 1878 to 1917 Japan experienced about a 2.3 percent annual agricultural growth. This increased productivity by 80 percent. During the same time the area of arable land expanded by 35 percent.[44] Independent India inherited a deformed socioeconomic structure and abyssmal poverty. Instead of using her limited resources to raise the educational and social level of the peasant, India embarked in industrialization. She accepted the simplistic theory that backwardness stems solely from lack of technological development. Referring to the post-1947 Indian development planning a scientist wrote:

> The approach towards technology and technological planning is . . . simplistic and bureaucratic. Science and technology, are looked upon, with a delicious confusion between the two and almost with a mystic religious faith, as the sole means of achieving this state of modernization. Given . . . budgetary allocations, different departments develop certain projects on an ad hoc basis and endeavor to achieve the financial targets. The concern for production achievements and accountability for success and efficiency is very limited. Comprehensive technological planning with optimal appropriate technological choices in [the] context of technological, economic, financial, social and environmental consideration is unknown.[45]

Both Japan and India were besieged by the West and its technological civilization. Without a typical colonial Western-educated intelligentsia, Japan fought the barbarians with their own weapons, while at the same time preserving the integrity of her society. The barbarians offered science and technology, and these Promethean gifts the Japanese adapted in the context of their institutions, especially those of the small agrarian household. In contrast to Japan, India was forced to come to terms with a threatening and swiftly changing world. India's Western-educated intelligentsia copied their masters so slavishly even after 1947 that they came to look at the Indian peasant with contempt. In the process they have accumulated the data of the arithmetic of poverty.

India has about 14 percent of the world's population. By the year 2000 India will have a population which will be four times that of the nineteenth century, about three times that of the 1950s and about double the current population. India has an average population density of 168/km^2 which is about eight times that of 22/km^2 in the United States. About 72 percent of the labor force is in agriculture. The average land holding is 0.7 hectares. A minority of 7 percent of the landowners possess 52 percent of the arable land while the smallest 25 percent of farmers own 1 percent of the land. The maldistribution of land is also reflected in the distribution of incomes. Undernourishment adds another factor in the equation of hunger. The average per capita calorie intake is about 2000. This is 83 percent of the United States

Department of Agriculture minimum allowance. As for the protein intake, it is only 49 grams, or 50 percent of the level in the United States. Only 6 out of the 49 grams are animal protein.[46] A 1967 document provides more facts of staggering implications for India's future:

> In "normal" times, between 50 and 75 percent of India's peoples do not have a balanced diet. Between 25 and 30 percent are *always* hungry. Persistent malnutrition means a burnt-out people, open to disease.
>
> Since independence, India's planners have poured their meager resources into industrial development. Agriculture, in a land of 600,000 villages dependent on the soil, has suffered. An awareness of a primacy of needs is growing; it may be too late.
>
> India carries a crippling war budget of 6 percent. Her real enemies are within her own borders and will not be conquered with guns.
>
> The size of the average farm is an inadequate two acres. Debt is endemic and the poor are at the mercy of the profiteer who buys their crops. The landless millions work larger holdings for a pittance.
>
> India loses a third of her harvest to rats, insects and to rot for lack of transport or storage facilities.
>
> For too long, in an age of technological possibilities, India's agriculture has been chained to the terrible bondage of the unpredictable monsoon cycle.
>
> Neglect of irrigation schemes, of wells and of water storage has brought growing misery to large areas. Crisis has pushed reams of paper plans off dusty government shelves and crash measures are now being undertaken, but many may pay with their lives for years of indifference or inactions.
>
> Interacting with all these massive problems are a tired land, hoarding and the non-cooperation between States, extensive corruption, a black market that penalizes the poor, the stick plow that barely breaks the soil, ignorance of modern farming methods, lack of pest control, of fertilizers and better seeds, vast herds of unproductive cattle, communal conflicts, indifference on too many government levels, a jungle of political parties, the iron inequities of the caste system, and a prevailing religious view which looks on human suffering as an inescapable fact of life. These are hard realities. They cannot be brushed away. All enter into the equations that add up to hunger.[47]

Despite these facts of hunger there is no reason why India must have a food problem. A nineteenth century student of India remarked that India had always produced enough food to feed its population. "The soil of India under irrigation never fails to produce a crop."[48] The future of India and that of Western knowledge to assist India to increase her food supplies lies in the hands of the Indian peasant. The peasant farmer of India needs more land and a material and social incentive to assure him that his labor and respect for the land contribute to national rather than to elite class prosperity. "There is no greater change agent in agriculture than an Indian farmer in hot pursuit of a rupee."[49] It is a great fallacy to assume that the traditional farmer is lethargic and against change. The Japanese farmer demonstrated the modernizing abilities of the traditional farmer. Clearly the traditional peasant farmer will become an agent of modernization only if he is shown the benefit of change and is given a chance. The Indian peasant must be given a chance if the Indian arithmetic of hunger is to change to an arithmetic of prosperity.

❈ *Chapter 2*

The American Elite and the Global Transfer of Agricultural Technology

GENESIS AND DEVELOPMENT OF THE GREEN REVOLUTION

The ability of the West to gain needed knowledge through scientific research has been the key to her affluence and power. Scientific discovery and technological innovation are closely connected. They led man to modernity. The demands of technology have been urgent in all phases of social life and political economy. "Technology is the social force of our time."[1] In the United States as of 1955 each dollar invested in hybrid corn research earned a very high annual profit in social returns.[2] The development of hybrid corn was "one of the outstanding technological successes of the century." Yet by itself hybrid corn was not a unique invention. It was rather "an invention of a method of inventing."[3]

It was this method of inventing that the Rockefeller Foundation scientists carried with them to Mexico when in 1943 they embarked on a long range cooperative scientific enterprise with the government of Mexico to improve the foodcrops of that country. The Rockefeller Foundation was invited to Mexico to solve the problem of low yields in the cultivation of corn, wheat, and beans. The foundation's program was incorporated in the institutional setting of Mexican agricultural research. And while this program experienced difficulties, it sustained its momentum without serious disruptions:

Land for experimental stations was pieced together plot by plot. Mexican officials required proof that commitments of resources were worth the

53

price. There were setbacks, as with the passing from the scene of key Mexican leaders at critical stages when their efforts might have assured accelerated progress. There was skepticism and even suspicion of highly qualified soil scientists and plant pathologists and of the style and vocabulary of strange breeds of agricultural scientists, such as agricultural economists. There was the brooding sense of uncertainty, even discouragement. . . . There were even temptations to lose sight of the axiom that it is more important to solve two or three problems than to fail with forty. There was recognition that there must be enough resources to support advances, but that sometimes it is good to be a little hungry because it forces the development of local resources.[4]

The work of the Rockefeller Foundation in Mexico unleashed the forces of an agricultural revolution in that country. The increase in food production was a noteworthy accomplishment. But the agricultural revolution brought more to Mexico than larger acre yields of corn, wheat, and beans. It helped the large Mexican farmer understand the material values of agricultural research. The farmer and the agronomist began to respect each other; and the agricultural scientist won the social standing formerly reserved for lawyers, engineers, and architects. The agricultural research program in Mexico brought together agricultural scientists of various American nations. But, above all, it contributed to the training and education of "an excellent corps of young Mexican scientists," and it helped to train scientists from other Latin American countries.[5] In short, the agricultural revolution in Mexico institutionalized a better management and understanding of the soils, animal production, and poultry husbandry. It was also responsible for the naturalization of a scientific attitude and tradition. The fact that agricultural science and technology had been successfully transferred to Mexico can be seen from the following observations made by two high Mexican officials in 1954:

> For the first time in my quarter century of service in the Ministry of Agriculture, I have heard Mexican investigators give Mexican extension men useful information derived from their own experiments. At last I have seen a group who had something of their own to tell and who know how to tell it.[6]

On February 22, 1959, during the inaugurating ceremonies of the postgraduate college of the National School of Agriculture, the Mexican minister of agriculture, Rodriguez Adame, made the following point:

> Today this national institute of higher learning in agriculture is completing 105 years of academic life. . . . The scientific and technologic

progress of the world during the past 100 years has necessitated the transformation of agriculture. . . . The days in which routine and empirical agriculture could be successful are definitely past. It is now a highly technical and complicated activity which requires the wise use of very extensive knowledge. Consequently, the technically trained man is a determining factor in the prosperity of all agricultural countries, and to discharge his obligation effectively it is essential that he be a professional with sound preparation and that he keep abreast of the very rapid progress in the various fields of agricultural sciences.[7]

The catalysts of increasing food production in Mexico were the high-yielding, dwarf foodcrop varieties. These food plants were designed, bred, and developed to combine a wide range of ecological adaptation, high genetic grain-yield potential, short straw, disease resistance and responsiveness, as well as efficiency in the use of heavy doses of fertilizers. These seeds were soon exported to other poor nations. Their cultivation resulted in spectacular increases in cereal grain production. In the late 1960s the term green revolution was used to describe those high-yielding varieties of foodcrops and their technology and production. This term has implied many things to many people. The fact that the term green revolution seems to convey the impression of a general revolution in yields per hectare for a great number of crops covering vast areas of the world has oversimplified and distorted the limited progress made in increasing the yields of wheat, rice and corn. As commonly understood, the usage of the term green revolution has been "premature, too optimistic, or too broad in scope."[8] Yet this term is here to stay. It is very appropriate since it emphasizes a revolution in agricultural techniques.[9]

Given the factors of sunlight, fertilizers, and water, the green revolution varieties respond with increased yields. They have short, stiff straws that enable them to avoid lodging because of their high-yielding capacity. The rice varieties also have stiff, erect leaves for maximum exposure to sunlight. In the tropics the intensity of light is a limiting factor in the yield of crops. The high-yielding rice plant is insensitive to the length of the day. This allows planting year around. And since these new rice varieties mature in about two-thirds of the time necessary for an indigenous rice plant, they can be harvested three times a year.

Chemical fertilizer was the fuel that powered the green revolution. A kilo of nitrogen would enable the old seed to increase its yield by ten kilos of additional grain. The same amount of fertilizer applied to a new seed results in 20 to 25 or more additional kilos of grain.[10] The green revolution seeds are also irrigation seeds. This means that the most expensive and valuable land must be used for the cultivation of these high-yielding varieties of crops. In Turkey the new wheat flourished not in the Anatolian plain but in the higher rainfall coastal region. Uncontrolled monsoon rains make it difficult for the new varieties to grow. It is only under irrigation that these new food plants prosper. It will be recalled that these irrigation seeds are also fertilizer seeds. When the fertilizer input is balanced with controlled water supplies, then growth in crop production follows.

The seeds of the green revolution have for the most part not reached the poor farmers. This disparity in beneficial participation was first documented in Mexico, where the green revolution was born. It was the affluent farmer who benefited most from the agricultural research of the Rockefeller Foundation in Mexico. But this research "has had little impact upon the practices of the hundred of thousands of small, poorly educated corn farmers who eke out their living from the poorer soils with undependable sources of water."[11] The two most basic reasons that made the new technology readily available to the larger growers reflect, first, political decisions to favor the rich and, second, demand of the new crop varieties for fertilizer and plentiful and controlled supplies of water. The Mexican experience of making the rich grow richer was repeated in Morocco. More than 80 percent of Morocco's farmers were simply left out of the benefits of the new food technology. The failure of the green revolution technologies to reach the small farmer did not prevent the small Rockefeler and Ford Foundation elite to develop the arrangements for the management and institutionalization of the monocropping technologies born in Mexico.

DIMENSIONS OF POWER

The American agricultural technical assistance elite is basically a small community of Rockefeller and Ford Foundation officers.[12] Theirs is the tradition of the green revolution—"an artifact depending on one's point of view but nevertheless still alive, and still doing well."[13] Theirs is also a rich heritage of agricultural scientific achievement and of a prosperous land. Some of them, like F.F. Hill of the Ford Foundation, a founding father of the green revolution, came from a farming background at a time when this was true for many who studied agricultural sciences in both Canada and the United States. According to Hill:

> Most of the agricultural scientists in these two countries, as late as 1935 I should think, had themselves grown up on farms. So had extension agents, almost without exception. This was my own background. Such persons had an intimate knowledge of all aspects of farming—

technological, economic, social and political. They knew how farmers thought and felt. They had themselves been farmers to age 18 or 19.[14]

The fact that this elite is an integral part of two institutions responsible for the creation and institutionalization of the green revolution technologies adds another dimension to the context from which they view underdevelopment and agricultural science and technology transfer. This dimension is one of power. They command the resources of two of the biggest American private philanthropic foundations. Their power also comes from long experience in technical assistance and institution building in the poor countries. An understanding, then, of this elite's strategy on agricultural technology transfer transcends academic curiosity. It goes to the heart of the contemporary condition of the flow of agricultural knowledge to the underdeveloped countries. It is pertinent here to note that this elite continues to allocate several millions of dollars each year to the international agricultural research network. They also shape the scientific methodology and goals of this program of global outreach.

INSTITUTES FOR INTERNATIONAL AGRICULTURAL RESEARCH

Global outreach or technical assistance to the national research systems is the special function of the international agricultural research center that institutionalized the green revolution. The most well-known of these institutes are the International Rice Research Institute (IRRI) in the Philippines founded in 1960 and the International Maize and Wheat Improvement Center (CIMMYT) in Mexico established in 1966. In 1969 the American elite leadership of these centers concluded

> that the development of technology for the developing regions of the world, the strengthening of national institutions, and the creation of international communities of effort on major problems probably could be achieved most rapidly and economically by extending and deepening the programs of the existing four international centers and by creation of any additional ones needed.[15]

Since 1969 five more centers were added to the network making a total of nine operational centers developing "significant new tools to reinforce national efforts."[16]

The international center is for all purposes the darling of the American agricultural technical assistance elite. The strategically located international agricultural research centers "are considered crucial to the acceleration of basic foodcrop production in some 80 food-deficit countries and to the improved standards of living of hundreds of millions of poverty-stricken farm families."[17] These centers, just like the universities of the rich countries, are developing better technologies:

> They have put together scientific management. They represent an institutional structure necessary to produce and speed up the creation of improved foodcrops. They are not intended as a substitute for national research systems. Their outreach activities are the building blocks of resistance to a disease. Whether or not such building blocks will be used depends on each poor country's resources.[18]

Moreover, "the scientists of these research institutes and their work are a paradigm to the poor countries. They demonstrate that agriculture is indeed a good way of life. The fact also that those scientists want their students to become better than themselves shows that they are doing a good job."[19] The international agricultural research institutes "filled a vacuum that the multinational corporations and the local governments neglected and left out of their priorities."[20] They also "represent the first effort to develop a global strategy for agricultural development."[21]

SCIENTIFIC AND INSTITUTIONAL PARADIGM

To a large extent the international agricultural research centers founded since 1960 are an evolutionary development of the nineteenth century experiment station. Like those colonial institutional structures, IRRI and other members of the global network were started by private, rich country organizations to do research in the poor, non-Western regions. Both the colonial experiment station and the 1960's international center did not confine their work to developing new varieties but they also facilitated the diffusion of technologies. Then and now the principle was and is well understood that the gains of better technologies tend to benefit the consumers of the improved product. The experiment station was designed to produce more and cheaper cash crops. It was clearly in the interests of the British, Dutch, Portuguese, and French to support that technological effort in their colonies. Their investments paid off handsomely. The contemporary international agricultural research center was a private American effort to increase the foodcrop supplies of the poor countries. Unlike the colonial experiment station, the technologies of the international center benefit for the most part a non-Western consumer.

The transfer of agricultural science and technology to the poor countries depends on the institutionalization of an elastic supply of adaptive research and development and on the management of an inelastic supply of scientific and technological talent. The critical limiting factor of technical manpower provides the context within which two other major constraints operate: (1) the capacity of the national research system is not sufficiently strong and mature to deal with the problems and potential of biological agricultural technology transfer, and (2) the existing national industrial capacity is not advanced to the point of naturalizing the imported mechanical technology.[22]

These constraints in the transfer of agricultural technology have become less formidable thanks to the establishment in the last decade and a half of the international agricultural research centers: "Establishment of these research training centers can be considered as an institutional innovation facilitating the transfer of an ecology-bound location-specific agricultural technology from temperate-zone developed countries to tropical-zone developing countries."[23]

Even transcending the impact of the new foodgrain technologies they developed, the international institutes appear to provide a paradigm in the organization of scientific resources that, if transferred to the poor countries, will have a salutary influence in the strengthening of the national research capability. This paradigm is in the systems approach to the problems of foodgrain production. The international centers have shown at least to a limited degree that a multidisciplinary team of scientists can adapt a new technology to local conditions. These centers have also established a set of linkages with regional, national, and developed country resource base institutions. Such communication networks facilitated the evolution of an institutional infrastructure that helps the international centers benefit to some degree from the resources of economies of scale. The same infrastructure strengthens the indigenous research systems.[24]

PROBLEM-ORIENTED METHODOLOGY

From the beginning the International Rice Research Institute's scientific methodology was problem-oriented. This procedure influenced the choice of selecting staff scientists and essentially set the limits of research and training. The problems of the large Asian rice farmer became the research projects of IRRI. At the same time a balance was maintained between the practical and the theoretical dimensions of rice research at the "complete plant science research institute devoted exclusively to rice." The problem-oriented methodology of IRRI was strengthened by the decision to approach the rice-growing problems as an international, interdisciplinary team of scientists working in integrated effort and scope. It was also recognized that major advances in rice research should not lead to complacency since rice exists in a complex biological system with ever-changing problems whose very complexity makes quick solutions impossible.[25] Not only did IRRI redesign the rice plant for the tropics but during its first decade (1962–1972) of scientific work this international agricultural research center made the following contributions to pure and applied science of the rice plant and its culture: IRRI scientists established that there is "a strong positive correlation between grain yield and the amount of solar energy received by the rice plant during the last 45 days before harvest." IRRI accumulated "the most complete set of information on the chemical kinetics and thermodynamics of submerged soils that exists in the world." IRRI is also unrivaled on its knowledge of the chemistry of the rice grain. Finally, IRRI has the world's most complete data on rice.[26]

The main impact of IRRI has been seen in the "pervasiveness of the new technology" it developed. This technology

> has brought hope and optimism to the rice-growing peoples of the world, a world previously convinced that not much could be done to improve their lot. Rice research workers and extension people in many countries have completely revised their attitudes toward the future; new goals of yield and production have been revealed to them. Many now see that the tropics offers the planet's greatest untapped resource for feeding mankind. Furthermore, this resource will have to be used to its limit before man has succeeded in controlling his numbers and averting disaster for his species.[27]

IRRI launched its international activities with its requests to numerous Asian rice scientists and officials for samples of seeds of Asian rice varieties. Slowly IRRI built a world collection of rice germ plasm which it continuously shares and enriches on a global basis. IRRI's rice symposia served the important purpose of bringing together leading authorities on rice research, and helped the institute to "focus its own research program on critical problems." There is a training program which is an integral part of the institute's research effort and of its international cooperative work. IRRI's ambition is to "train the trainer" in both rice production and theory. Several key rice breeders of Korea, Ceylon, Indonesia, Pakistan, Bangladesh, and India received their training at IRRI. From 1964 when IRRI initiated its production training to 1971, the institute guided the individual in residence training or independent study of 657 production-oriented specialists from 40 countries.[28] The Ford Foundation made funds available to IRRI to foster international cooperative research. IRRI symposia helped to generate cooperative projects which, in addition to their scientific contributions, "led to long standing inter-agency ties." The travel of IRRI scientists to Asian rice-producing countries was another important dimension in the internationalization of the institute's activities. It facilitated the institute's outreach potential; that is, it made possible for IRRI to embark on research, planning, and assistance designed to strengthen rice research and production in other countries. Each outreach project involved the national agency, a funding organization, and IRRI. A formal agreement or understanding between these three parties provided the needed frame of reference for the specific project:

> The basic philosophy of these agreements was clear on an important point: they were in no sense intended to lead to the establishment of branch stations of the International Rice Research Institute. Rather, they were designed to foster improvements in the host countries' research and development programs. The degree and pace of IRRI's involvement would be set by the decisions of local authorities and the work would be directed solely towards problems of concern to local rice scientists and rice farmers.[29]

Since 1965 IRRI's outreach or "country programs" contributed to the improvement of rice production in Bangladesh, Pakistan, India, Ceylon, Indonesia, Thailand, South Korea, South Vietnam, Philippines, Burma, Malaysia, and Taiwan.[30] The fact that IRRI developed successful cooperative projects with these Asian countries indicated that IRRI as a research institute provides a mechanism flexible enough to respond to special ecological conditions and rich in expertise to produce concrete results.

RESEARCH AND TRAINING

IRRI is basically a research institute. The research project constitutes the core of its training methodology. The "major objective of the project approach is to provide participants with a solid research experience—teaching them each step involved in planning, designing, executing and reporting on a research project."[31] And like the CIMMYT trainees, those of IRRI returned to their national research systems to modernize rice research and production programs. The graduates of both institutes absorbed not merely knowledge but the scientific ethic or normative structure of IRRI and CIMMYT. The poor country scientists selected by IRRI were better educated than those of CIMMYT. They also continued to put heavy emphasis on knowledge-generating research activities upon their graduation.[32] The relatively young life of IRRI and CIMMYT makes it possible to assume that above all their philosophies were shaped by the small group of senior American scientists who institutionalized the working methodology of the two centers. The fact that IRRI has become a graduate school is no doubt a reflection of the twelve year leadership of Robert F. Chandler who joined IRRI directly from college research. CIMMYT's major concern with farmer problems again mirrors Norman E. Borlaug's nonacademic, practical approach to raising food production.[33] This explains why more than 50 percent of the IRRI graduates prefer academic teaching or research while most of the CIMMYT trainees focus on wheat improvement once back home.

CIMMYT trains selected members of the national research systems precisely in order to bring about organizational changes within those systems. Certainly lack of efficient research methodology is a limiting factor in poor country agricultural research. But what CIMMYT seems to consider very serious is the normative structure of developing country agricultural research systems, especially those procedures dealing with practical, problem-solving research, hard field work, and close cooperation with the farmer. In order to redirect national wheat teams to solving farmer problems, CIMMYT follows the strategy of training a minimum "critical mass" of researchers within each national program. The idea behind this strategy is simple. CIMMYT wants the national wheat program to be structured after its own "aggressive, farmer-oriented, practical, problem-solving approach to wheat improvement." This can be accomplished with a sufficient number of CIMMYT-trained research workers within the national program.[34] About 91.2 percent of the former CIMMYT trainees remained actively involved in wheat research in their national agricultural research systems. What is more, they also moved into senior level positions in the administrative structure of those systems.[35]

Both IRRI and CIMMYT have demonstrated that they have the capacity to discover or produce both new technologies and new technical and engineering knowledge. They achieved technical excellence by their effective utilization of imaginative administrative and research support. They also were fortunate to have access to conceptual-scientific skills in their research programs. Needless to say, the fact that the national research systems in the tropics and subtropics lacked both the scientific and administrative potential for distinction made IRRI and CIMMYT all the more dominant in agricultural research. "In a crude sense, the 'main' stations in national research programs have become 'branches' to either CIMMYT or IRRI." Such a development was perhaps inevitable given the dependence of the national experiment stations on the rice and wheat international centers for both foodcrop varieties and genetic materials. The international breeding program of CIMMYT reinforces even further the existing hierarchical structure of international agricultural research. This breeding program has built-in incentives "for a simple service-oriented hierarchy."[36]

KNOWLEDGE TRANSFER AND DIFFUSION
OF TECHNOLOGIES

The International Rice Research Institute developed rice technologies that have expanded the potential for growth of the tropical rice economies. In contrast to tropical national research systems, IRRI did not have a bureaucracy-ridden research program. Its progress was made possible by its high quality intellectual capital with all the benefits of Japanese and, in general, temperate zone knowledge and experience. IRRI had the resources to reward both the intellectual and material needs of its scientists.

The establishment of IRRI in 1960 came at a time when the diffusion of improved Japanese rice varieties to Taiwan had resulted in the development of the genetic stock from which the green revolution was born. What IRRI did was simply to utilize effectively the impressive intellectual resources at its command. Knowledge diffusion in this context was bound to occur. What is surprising, however, is the fact that since 1966 when IRRI scientists developed IR-8, the institute's first rice variety, there has been an apparent diminution in the incremental discoveries by the center's researchers. "Essentially, no gain in real yielding ability over IR-8 has been forthcoming to date." No doubt advances have taken place but these are in the improved grain quality, disease and insect resistance, and related technologies of the rice plant.

The early dissemination of rice varieties was widespread. Such a diffusion of IRRI technologies

> was accelerated by the fact that a number of international agencies were in jeopardy of severe embarrassment because of their own unimaginative programs to develop technology and desperately needed to get on the green revolution "bandwagon." There was then a major push to diffuse the green revolution varieties. In fact, however, in spite of the propaganda about day length insensitivity, the IRRI varieties were quite sensitive to soil and climate factors, especially as regards water availability and control. These factors would probably have been

sufficient to limit the diffusion of the new varieties to perhaps 20 percent or so of the Asian tropical rice producing region. The "adaptive" research programs *and* the continued development of the national research programs, which were underway before IRRI, have resulted in an expanded set of high yielding varieties and extended the green revolution.[37]

Today we are paying a price for the optimism of the 1960s—the heyday of the green revolution. "The premise of progress through science no longer commands the attention of a few years ago."[38]

TECHNOLOGIES FOR THE SMALL PEASANT FARMER

A political strategy is by necessity a plan designed to achieve some well-defined development goals. A strategy for agricultural modernization is, then, a plan for social change. It must, above all, be based on historical reality. The outcome of an agricultural strategy will be determined as much by population growth and natural resources as by social structures and political economy. The social component of agricultural technology transfer is an issue to which the American agricultural technical assistance elite is slowly giving more theoretical attention. Apparently it took the publication of Theodore W. Schultz's *Transforming Traditional Agriculture* in 1964[39] to convince this elite that not all farmers are handcuffed by tradition. What Schultz said was hardly new. Yet his book became the "bible" of Sterling Wortman—a powerful member of this elite. Schultz's *Transforming Traditional Agriculture* also triggered the Puebla Project.[40] This project was an experiment designed to transfer the new CIMMYT technologies to 47,600 small, 2.5 hectare farmers cultivating rain-fed corn land in the Puebla State of Mexico. It cost the Rockefeller Foundation about $1.1 milion to support this technology transfer project between 1967 and 1973.[41] The project faced several problems. The fertilizers distributed by the government were of the wrong formulas. Credit agencies were unwilling to lend money to farmers with less than 15 acre farms. Some innovation followed to change these practices. In general, the political and economic organization and lack of support by government agencies hindered the growth of the Puebla Plan. Yet this experiment did demonstrate the technical and economic feasibility of technology transfer and farmer adoption of that technology. The Puebla Project benefited 12,000 farmers.[42]

We do not know whether the Puebla Plan was responsible for the fact that the American agricultural technical assistance elite is today interested in the welfare of the farmer in the poor countries:

[I]n many instances the farmers have developed rather successful production systems within the framework of resources available to them. In
other cases, the systems evolved by farmers are difficult to improve upon
even with so-called advanced technology. Sometimes "technology" con-
sists of the "discovery" of practices commonly used by farmers themselves . . . we have to begin with the farmer. We need to know his
production constraints; we need to understand his motivation, and we
need to give him a fair return for his efforts. The farmer must have
confidence in the systems and the people who are supposed to assist
him.[43]

The small peasant farmer of the poor countries has for centuries
earned a minimal income from the meager returns of his long-
impoverished tiny farm. For the most part this peasant farmer lives in
areas remote from centers of commerce. His income is so abysmally low
that he is essentially beyond the reach of development and political
economy. He is usually malnourished and has little access to education, health, and other social services. The small peasant farmer is still
a subsistence farmer.[44] In Brazil, for instance, most of the poor are to
be found in agriculture. "Of all Brazilian men, ten years and older,
who were part of the labor force and made less than four dollars a
month in 1970, 85.5 percent worked in agriculture and 83.7 percent
were unskilled agricultural workers. These are the poor." The urban
poor are not as poor as those living in the rural areas. The metropolitan poor at least have access to social services like schooling for their
children and housing facilities. "The rural poor are mainly landless
agricultural workers, share-croppers, and *minifundistas*, who work a
piece of land so small that it is insufficient to absorb their labor and
that of their families."[45]

Concerned for the small peasant farmer of the underdeveloped
countries and knowing precisely what appropriate green revolution
technologies mean to this farmer, the foundation agricultural elite
rightly maintains that when new technology fails to be accepted, it is
not because the poor country farmer is illiterate or superstitious.
Rather,

nonadoption probably occurs because of the incompleteness or unprofita-
bility of the recommended technology, or because of the farmer's inability to take advantage of useful technology owing to unavailability of
inputs, unfavorable prices, or lack of access to a dependable market.
Thus, when farmers fail to adopt new practices, the fault will lie most
often, not with them, but with the scientists, the economists, the national
leaders, and private industry.[46]

F.F. Hill of the Ford Foundation put the above thesis in this way:

For a technology to be transferred it needs to be better than the existing variety. And while scientists know more about biological technologies it is the farmers who know more about the risk involved in accepting those technologies. No technology can move ahead without the availability of physical inputs like fertilizers and the institutional arrangements like credit and price. The farmer of the poor countries is intelligent. He knows how to count. In order that he takes the risk to adopt a new technology that technology has to be better than the existing traditional farming methods.[47]

NATIONAL AGRICULTURAL RESEARCH

The major function of the international agricultural research center is that of outreach, i.e., those activities of the centers designed to be of assistance to agricultural research and development on a global scale. This primarily means that "it is in the context of the global network of agricultural research that technology transfer takes place."[48] So far technology has moved from the centers to the national research systems. The emergence in the poor countries of the experiment station or research center as an adaptive and development mechanism for new technology has been a critical element in the international transfer or "naturalization" of agricultural technology.[49] Yet this national mechanism for the naturalization of imported technology has suffered from the overall weakness of the national research systems, to the point where the international community, and especially the American agricultural technical assistance elite, sponsored a conference in 1974 on how to strengthen national agricultural research systems.[50] The conclusion of this conference is not flattering to the potential of indigenous agricultural institutions to solve their own problems: "None of the developing countries can be said to have a program of sufficient size to do the job ahead."[51]

Poor countries do not appreciate the scope and depth needed in agricultural research. They understand that experiment stations, national laboratories and colleges of agriculture are the proper institutional setting for agricultural research. But what they do not understand is that new technologies have to be tested at each farming region and, most important of all, "at the ultimate experimental site—the individual farm." The farmer, then, is left to his own capabilities. The scientific establishment of the poor country assumes that activities leading to the adoption of new technologies by the farmer is beyond its responsibility. This has left the farmer with the extension worker to solve the complex issues of technological adaptation, management, and economic inputs for specific environmental situations. But the extension worker is usually limited both in his formal education and in his inexperience in technical farming. Without training and continuous access to new technology and without a formal association with the research establishment, the extension worker in the poor countries is "relatively useless" in serving the cause of the farmer or of modern agriculture.[52]

The elitist and misguided attitude of the poor country agricultural research establishment toward technology adaptation and its acceptance by the farmer is reflected in the agricultural college and the purposes it serves. And it is not surprising to learn that a major barrier to progress within the agricultural college is the same faculty member who refuses to have anything to do with either the extension worker or the farmer. Frequently the professor or research scientist is simply incapable of using the limited library resources at his disposal. If he is not outside the mainstream of scientific thought, he is likely to write articles on topics relevant to rich countries. Teaching at the undergraduate level at the national universities is equally dismal. "Too often professors have been cut off from new ideas and new procedures. Their teaching is outdated, dry, irrelevant, and according to textbooks rather than common sense approaches."[53] The student who enters the agricultural college or university does not have much of a chance that he will learn something of immediate use for the welfare of the farmers living near the agricultural school:

> [S]tudents at agricultural colleges in developing nations usually have little opportunity while in college to develop a real proficiency in crop, soil, or animal management. It also is not unusual for example, to find that a college faculty member who is teaching a course in crop management is not himself able to grow a good crop.[54]

Agricultural research in the poor countries is basically irrelevant to local needs. Foreign-educated underdeveloped country agricultural scientists tend to work on problems that have very little to do with the conditions of their agricultural economies.[55] This is because the agricultural systems and scientists of those low-income regions are vainly attempting to compete with their former tutors. In this misdirected effort they usually explore issues useful to the rich nations but totally useless to their own tropical and subtropical environments.[56] It need not be emphasized that in this context the needs of the local farmers are ignored. Praiseworthy as the effort to advance the frontiers of the rich nations' knowledge may be, at this critical juncture in history such an approach "is a luxury poor countries cannot afford."[57]

In the period from 1950 to 1970, both rich and poor countries invested considerably in public sector research, especially in their efforts to improve the efficiency of crop and livestock production. In global terms these 20 years witnessed a fourfold increase in real investment. The 1950s allowed for a rapid expansion in the rich nations' agricultural research systems while a similar growth was repeated in the 1960s among the developing regions. Poor countries increased their funding of agricultural research from about 10 percent in the 1950s to nearly 13 percent in 1965 and to more than 15 percent by 1970.[58] In the 1950s and 1960s underdeveloped nations paid heavily for the then current premise that extension was an integral component of technology transfer. They spent 1.2 times as much on extension as they did on research, considerably more than the corresponding investment of the technology-exporting countries. It cost the poor country 6.7 times as much to support one research scientist as it did to pay the salary of one extension worker. This reflects as much the low level of education and skills of the extension worker as the scarcity of scientific talent. When the international scientist dominates the national research system, as for instance in Africa and the Middle East, he commands funding and expenditures that are about as lavish as those in the developed nations. The international agricultural research centers spend close to $100,000 per scientist per year. No less expenditures are necessary to pay for the scientific resources per international scientist at a national agricultural research center.[59]

In 1965 there were about 10,000 agricultural scientists in the poor countries. A large number of these scientists were subsidized to study at the universities of the rich nations. At the same time large numbers of scientists from the developed regions taught at the underdeveloped nation universities or built the agricultural research capabilities of these schools. Today the number of international scientists working at the national research systems has been drastically reduced from the 1950s level. There has also been a drastic decline of the international financial support to national systems. It is now the international agricultural research center that has become the beneficiary of the aid flow to agricultural research.[60]

Technical and engineering skills are not a scarce commodity in the underdeveloped countries. It is the technical-scientific skills that are in very limited supply, while conceptual scientific skills are practically nonexistent in some poor countries. Where the technical and engineering skills are the dominant resources of an agricultural research system, the experiment stations are widely diffused and in approach they tend to be commodity-oriented. With little real capacity to design flexible and changing methodology these stations conduct experiments and field trials that in essence do not differ much from the "cook-book" procedure. These experiment stations are small and they rarely maintain strong working relations with advanced graduate teaching institutions. With only technical and engineering capabilities, the poor country agricultural research system and experiment stations only can direct their limited potential to adapt technology produced by others. The technological and biological context of agricultural technology makes such a technology sensitive to soil, climate, and various economic factors. Ideally each "ecological niche" could have its unique set of technologies. Yet agricultural research systems are not designed to tailor technologies to minor niches. They are also not capable to adapt technologies at the rate they are created. This means that a lot of technology transfer never takes place.[61] Moreover, technology adaptation is a costly process.[62]

The indigenous research capability of a country is one of the major factors that determines the success or failure of technology transfer.

[C]ountries without the capacity to produce internationally significant research publications, also lacked the capacity to benefit from the research findings of other countries. Extension and related programs did not facilitate transfer. Those countries which did have indigenous research capability in wheat and maize production, benefited significantly from the research done in other similar regions, but *not* from research conducted outside those regions. For example, research findings are not transferred from temperate climate zones to tropical climate zones.[63]

SOCIAL DIMENSION OF TECHNOLOGY TRANSFER

This brief analysis of the technology transfer philosophical premises of the American agricultural technical assistance elite shows that the technical component—the generation of better technologies—and its embodiment in the international center network dominate the thinking, action, and resources of these men. The reality they represent cannot be easily challenged. The centers they founded and continue to assist and guide are definitely needed by the underdeveloped countries. The national research systems can be strengthened if supporting national policies are designed. The centers also represent a form of international cooperation that has the seeds for evolution:

International cooperation in agriculture has reached a level that is spectacularly superior to anything attained in the past, in that a mechanism now exists for actual development of technology. Although several of the international agricultural research centers are very new, the network which they comprise represents one of the most comprehensive efforts ever undertaken to upgrade agricultural technology. In concept, it equals in scope and vigor anything undertaken in agricultural research in the past within the advanced nations. There has been nothing remotely comparable to it in the tropical environment.[64]

Developing technology as they do, the centers are also the major mechanism for the transfer of their technologies. But that is all they can do. And yet technology transfer has a social dimension that even transcends the development of technology itself. This social dimension was partially revealed as a major constraint in the transfer of technology to the poor countries in the context of those countries' archaic agricultural research systems. The social component of technology transfer, then, concerns man's relations to his social cosmos and necessarily to the uses of technology at his command.

Werner Kiene of the Ford Foundation put the social dimension of agricultural technology transfer into a classic formulation. He said:

> Prices must reflect the potential of the poor countries. Technology has to fit into that context. National policies must permit prices to a level that makes sense. Farmers can then benefit. *Dramatic social changes are necessary in the underdeveloped countries for the good use of technology and.for good food production.* (Emphasis mine.)[65]

A. Colin McClung of the Rockefeller Foundation made the point that the rate of technology transfer to Asia is reduced by the willingness of the Asian establishment to maintain the existing forms of social inequality in that continent.[66] It appears, then, that the elite these two foundation officers represent is concerned with the social implications of technological change. And the same elite continues to propound that the fate of the small peasant farmer in the poor countries is becoming "an important conscious priority" in the international agricultural research system. Technologies are exclusively designed to benefit the poor farmer.[67] However, there is an abyss of difference between this assertion and the actual fact. What follows will show that whatever technologies flow from the international network are definitely not designed to benefit the poor farmer.

TECHNOLOGY TRANSFER CONSTRAINTS: TECHNOLOGICAL AND SOCIAL

Technology transfer is a two-way street. Information is generated at one point but it must be delivered to another. Technology transfer is also a two-dimensional process. The technical component may reach the farmer as a complete package:

By "complete packages" is meant high-yielding varieties, plus appropriate fertilizer-use techniques, plus adequate means of control of diseases and insect pests, plus necessary planting, cultivation, and irrigation techniques—any and all of which, combined, permit the high yield. Or, in the case of animals, it means proper strain, nutrition, and management—all at once, with nothing important left out.[68]

Even if the farmer can effectively utilize his package of technology there are other major constraints in the underdeveloped countries in the path of agricultural technology transfer. One of these constraints is related to national policies. John A. Pino of the Rockefeller Foundation put this issue in the following context:

The fact of the matter is that it is not the lack of technology which impedes production (though we recognize this need) but rather the existence of inadequate policies, the lack of adequate policies or the ineffective implementation of policies. Thus we have come to feel that the weakest link in the production system is the national institutional complex, i.e., the capacity to develop efficient production systems and convey these to the farmer, to get them accepted, adopted, and put to use.[69]

Dale E. Hathaway of the Ford Foundation goes even further in his assessment of constraints in agricultural technology transfer to the poor countries. Agriculture in the less developed countries (LDCs)

is plagued with massive underemployment, human and capital resources with low productivity, and antiquated technology. Thus, the supply curve for farm products is highly inelastic due to physical constraints, and increases in supply can come only from the expansion of cultivated area or adoption of new technology by millions of illiterate or semiliterate peasant farmers. Moreover, since most of the new technologies are land saving but capital using (high-yielding seeds, fertilizers, pesticides, and so on) and require skilled management, they are in most cases adopted slowly and only in the few areas where credit, risk, and management conditions allow. Thus, the Green Revolution, as it is commonly understood, is not won. The battle plans are still being formed. Despite their difficulties in expanding agricultural output, the underdeveloped countries have sacrificed the price incentive needed to speed the adoption of new technology to pursue a cheap food policy for their urban consumers. Over much of the period from 1955 to 1970, the leaders in the LDCs were abetted in those policies by the large-scale provision of "surplus" grains generated by the excess capacity in developed countries, which was provided generously by the United States under the Food for Peace program of the Agricultural Trade Development and Assistance Act of 1954 (Public Law 480), and by other countries via various price-cutting devices.[70]

The transfer of agricultural science and technology to the underdeveloped countries is clearly a fragile enterprise. The technological component of this enterprise in the flow of knowledge is crucial. But unless the poor nations put their house in order there is not much of a chance that technology can really benefit the millions of illiterate peasants who need it most. Hathaway put this complex technological, social issue of technology transfer into a proper perspective:

> Technology for Asia is mainly rice. The adaptation and utilization of this technology depends primarily on the existing environmental and institutional structures. For instance, water control is essential to rice technology. And yet in Asia only 20 percent of rice production benefits from controlled water supplies. Water control is an integral part of investment and institutional problems like the pricing of the inputs. There may be a lot of water available but energy is a major constraint in terms of utilization of various resources. The illiterate peasant is usually offered a package of practices. But this package is either unavailable or it is too expensive with the result that farmers revert to old practices. Technological packages require credit hence credit systems are developed to serve the farmer. But such systems fail to work because of inept administration, the delivery process is too cumbersome and because of the corruption of those who manage the credit agencies. With no flexibility toward the farmer these institutions are no better than moneylenders. The credit systems of the underdeveloped countries are designed to keep people from stealing rather than make them work—still the colonial mentality intact. The British left to their former colonies a legacy of an administrative structure that was designed to avoid change. Such a structure was certainly not intended to promote development. It trains people for the wrong thing, only for civil service. Poor countries lack a system of apprenticeship so that even in rural areas students are prepared for college but without practical or agricultural experience. The fact is that in most of the underdeveloped nations the concept of service and research is basically nonexistent. When research does exist then it is separated from its social functions. And these poor countries have an absolutely lousy educational system to prepare them to use technology or development. In Asia and Latin America the colonial past and mentality are still dominant. Africa in this regard is better off since the colonial institutional structures left behind are fragile. The Africans, then, have the opportunity to build their own institutions. In the underdeveloped countries social sciences play no role in the decision-making process. But above all it is the philosophy of science that is a major constraint in the transfer of agricultural technology and science to the poor regions of the globe. The whole philosophy of science is Western and it is intertwined with religious concepts and values. Non-Western people do not believe that man can solve those problems not under his control. Hence, science is not considered as a proper solution to man's problems. Top underde-

veloped country scientists educated in the West do consult their astrologers before traveling. The one non-Western country to have exploited its resources is China. People is the best resource that any country has. China is the only society to have effectively utilized its resources. With natural and human resources a good share of the underdeveloped world can make it.[71]

Hathaway's is a balanced synthesis of the technological and social components of technology transfer. Its force and clarity reflect knowledge and experience that result from direct contact with the brutal realities of underdevelopment. We do not know whether the other members of the technical assistance elite share Hathaway's views entirely. Hathaway's point about China was also made by Sterling Wortman of the Rockefeller Foundation.

THE CHINESE COLLECTIVIST PARADIGM

In late 1974 a U.S. Plant Sciences Delegation headed by Wortman visited China for a month. These nine plant scientists and a historian had the opportunity to see and observe various agricultural research institutes, agricultural colleges, and five communes. What they saw may or may not be representative of Chinese rural development and agriculture. Yet, like other visitors to China, they were impressed and surprised by the evidence they examined. According to Wortman, the crops looked good, productivity seemed uniformly good, and "in a sense there is no farming in China—even the grain crops are 'gardened'." Wortman also pointed out that Chinese scientists and technicians are directly involved with the peasant and his problems. Wortman concluded that China does have the potential and the right attitudes for development and growth: "One does not sense the hopelessness evident in some other countries. Rather, there is a hope for a better future."[72]

China is indeed one of the few societies that managed to effectively utilize its human resources with a minimum dependence on technology. And this she accomplished with a population of 850 million people and without any substantial assistance from the prosperous West. Even Russia in the late 1950s ordered its technicians home from China. The key to China's self-sufficiency must be seen in that society's organization to permit an equal distribution of responsibilities and limited resources. As it still is a peasant society, China put a top priority in the transformation of her agriculture. China does not have a food problem or the other major problems of the underdeveloped countries because she mobilized not merely all of her intellectual resources but above all she made her society work by the labor of human feet and hands.

There is no doubt that as mankind is threatened by the problems of scarcity and global poverty, the Chinese collectivist challenge will increasingly become more profound for both the West and the underdeveloped world. The Chinese did pay perhaps a high human price for their social order and discipline. It is here, then, in the question of human freedom that the Chinese paradigm provides an even greater challenge to those concerned with human development and global poverty:

> But the real answer to the collectivist challenge will not be found in the realms of doctrine or of theory. To give the Chinese their due, their solutions did not spring fullblown from Marxist-Leninist dogma, even as modified by Chairman Mao Tse-tung. They were worked out step by painful step within the framework of their particular vision. And with all their faults and shortcomings, visitors give them credit for evolving a more or less egalitarian society geared to the fair sharing of scarcity.[73]

It appears that the American agricultural technical assistance elite, however narrowly defined in this chapter, provides the technological context for the transfer of agricultural science and technology to the poor countries. The strength of this elite is in its financial resources, in the international center network, and in the ideas of its members. This elite argues that the major constraints in the transfer of the technology generated by the centers are to be found in the scientific and, above all, the social institutional structure of the underdeveloped countries.

One of these centers is located in Colombia, a classic paradigm of backwardness, precarious food needs, and underdevelopment. Do the "better" technologies of this international institute reach the small farmer of Colombia? The next two chapters will take a close look at this question. In a real sense the technical assistance philosophy of the American elite will be moved from the esoteric realms of theory to the brutal facts of poverty. And since in Colombia poverty and agricultural resources are controlled by a few men of privilege and wealth, it is pertinent here that a brief point be made about the structure of the elites these men represent. Who then are the Colombian elites?

> At this time they are the leaders of the Liberal and Conservative political parties, the "conservative" military which is not uninclined to use force and torture, and the chief entrepreneurs in industry and agribusiness. The church does not appear to be as influential as ever, but it can exert pressure on issues involving the morals of the other elites. Family links between the elites are not clear, nor is it evident that they strive for similar aims and objectives. What seems to hold them up, however, is the prospect that if one of them falls, they will all collapse together . . . they

realize they are mutually reinforcing elements. In the simplest sense, the rich are needed to pay for the personal activities of political leaders. The political leaders, in turn, try to maintain good international relations for markets of select Colombian products. Political leaders also serve to address the problems of the poor sufficiently "to keep the lid on the boiling kettle." The military gives legitimacy to the government and tries to arrest the problems of violence.[74]

Chapter 3

Colombia's Predicament with Technology, Rural Poverty, and Rural Violence: Backwardness and the Pathology of Fear

VIOLENCE AND THE RURAL POOR OF COLOMBIA

Colombia's twentieth century history is above all stained in the blood of the peasant poor. In 1928, 23,000 banana plantation workers organized a strike against the United Fruit Company. The conservative Colombian government responded to this protest by an army massacre of hundreds of the workers and their families. Twenty years later the same system assassinated Jorge Eliécer Gaitán, a lawyer whose sole crime was to have defended the poor and to have united the dispossessed masses against the elite. This time the people of Bogotá stormed the citadels of the conservative elite. They burned their own city, they slaughtered, and they were themselves slaughtered. Again this bloodbath ended, but without a victory for the poor. The liberal elite placated the masses for the simple reason that the pact they extracted from the frightened conservatives brought them to power. But the conservatives' reign of terror of the rural poor continued. This is how a contemporary witness put it:

My eyes have seen many sights. I have seen men coming into the cities mutilated, women raped, children flogged and wounded. I saw a man whose tongue had been cut out, and people who were lashed to a tree and made to witness the cruel scene told me that the policemen yelled, as they cut out his tongue: 'You won't be giving any more cheers for the Liberal Party, you bastard!' They cut the genitals off other men so that they wouldn't procreate any more Liberals. Others had their legs and arms cut off and were made to walk about, bleeding, on the stumps of

77

their limbs. And I know of men who were bound while policemen and Conservative citizens took it in turns to rape their wives and daughters. Everything was carried out according to a preconceived plan of extermination. And the victims of these bloodthirsty policemen were poor, humble country people who were members of the Liberal Party. Their wives, their old folk, and their children were shot in the full light of day. The official police took possession of the property of the Liberal farmers, killed their owners, requisitioned their barns and disposed of their money, their livestock; in a word, of all that had been the livelihood of their families. It was an avalanche of pillage and an orgy of blood. At times these atrocious crimes were committed under the cover of night, with the encouragement of high government officials. And all this in the false name of God, with holy medals jingling around their necks, and without remorse.[1]

In the cities this rural upheaval was called *Violencia*. It brought to the countryside "an avalanche of pillage and an orgy of blood." The Colombian rural society was consumed by violence. The Indians lost more and more of their land. Various landlords organized private small armies to throw the peasants off their properties. Meanwhile the Conservative party in 1949 imposed a reign of terror and declared the state of siege throughout Colombia. This was followed by an extensive civil war fought in the countryside. The peasants paid dearly in this fratricidal upheaval. They killed each other and saw their lands occupied, their houses burned, and their crops confiscated. Since 1964 rural violence in Colombia has merely subsided. *Haciendas* are still invaded by migrant peasants. The Indians have few mountain or jungle refuges in which they have a reasonable hope to escape death. In December 1967, six Colombian cowboys invited several nomadic Indians to a Christmas party. In the course of the festivities the Indians were massacred because the cowboys "did not know it was a crime to kill Indians."[2] And in June 1975 the Liberal President Alfonso López Michelsen of Colombia imposed a state of siege in an attempt to crush rural "discontent arising from poverty and social injustice."[3]

THE COLOMBIAN RURAL ELITE

The rural elite of Colombia has for the past four centuries used force to maintain its dominance over the fragile social and political order that continued and expanded the mandate of the Spanish conquest. Numerous peasant uprisings have always been the greatest challenge to the monopoly of power and wealth of the landed elite. The old order is equally threatened by a rapid population growth and by a technological revolution. Colombia is likely to have 50 million people by the turn of this century. This internal demographic revolution cannot but have explosive consequences in a static environment. And while the technological revolution has no roots in Colombia, its impact has already begun to change the physical and intellectual frontiers of that country and its people.

Land has been the source of power and wealth in Colombia. The majority in the agricultural sector is still living in a subsistence rural economy. Institutionalized land tenure inequalities permit the small rural elite to use the landless agricultural workers as labor in return for a wage of perpetual poverty. The landholder, or *patron,* has both the state and local resources at his command. In a way he is the community. Within his very large estate (*latifundio*), his word is law. Everything functions at his discretion and good will. And within the broader community his patronage is essential for social services. Business institutions operate largely for his convenience.

RURAL POVERTY

The "massive exodus" of the rural population of Colombia from agriculture to the cities reflects the desperate effort of the peasants to escape the crushing poverty of their social and physical environment. The Colombian rural majority has "vastly inferior" basic facilities like water and health care. The children of the peasants can for the most part aspire to no more that two years of elementary schooling. And since 3.5 percent of the rural elite owns two-thirds of all farmland, the average Colombian peasant, if he owns land at all, has a farm of extremely small size.[4]

In 1960 more than 750,000 Colombian peasant families cultivated farms of less than two hectares. There were also 175,000 families who neither owned nor operated any land. Together these peasant families made up about 70 percent of the rural people of Colombia and 40 percent of the total population. Most of the small farm units represented no more than one-fourth of the cultivated land and are located in mountainous regions—by itself a major environmental constraint to agricultural development. Eighteen thousand landlords owned nearly 46 percent of the land while more than one million of the small farmers owned no more than 6 percent of the farm land.[5] Meanwhile the number of landless families in Colombia was increasing at 10 percent per year.[6]

The Colombian rural elite does not merely control the resources of agricultural investment but is the chief beneficiary of technical assistance and rural infrastructure. Large landowners also have unlimited access to institutional credit.[7] In Colombia credit is available on the basis of "creditworthiness" alone and is apparently unrelated to the expected investment returns:

> This, unfortunately, excludes many farmers capable of executing sound investment programs and is partly responsible for the skewed size distribution of loans. Greater emphasis on credit coupled with technical services would help introduce modern production practices into much of Colombian agriculture, where lack of technical know-how is the greatest factor limiting rapid expansion of output. The agricultural sector cannot reasonably expect to increase further its share of total lending, so if agricultural output growth is to be accelerated, technology and credit will have to be regarded as mutually dependent inputs. Harnessing credit as the instrument to induce modernization of Colombian agriculture is the great challenge facing the government and banking system.[8]

No doubt this institutionalized rural inequality is responsible both for the maldistribution of land resources and for low agricultural productivity. The vast rural majority works in a context that inhibits the utilization of its work capacity. At the same time the rural elite that holds most of the land provides gainful employment to a small number of agricultural workers. Cultivating as they do one-fourth of the farmland the small Colombian peasant farmers manage to produce two-thirds of all output in the agricultural sector.[9] And yet the gross income of the small farmer is between 0.1 and 2 percent of the gross returns of the average member of the rural elite. The poor peasant spends roughly 50 to 90 percent of his modest cash receipts to buy food. It is hardly surprising that in this context of poverty the poor Colombian peasant is also a victim of inadequate nutrition:

> In Colombia, where one can find a cross-section of the food problems besetting much of Latin America, nutrition-related diseases claim two of every five children who die before the age of 6. At a hospital in Bogotá, I saw rows of cribs holding pathetically shrunken figures, each 35 or 40 percent under normal size, suffering from edema and pellagra, and blotched with body sores. These were victims of chronic malnutrition.[10]

GARCIA ROVIRA: INTEGRATED RURAL DEVELOPMENT?

It is recognized increasingly that "[a]t the root of the world's food problems are serious imbalances in the availability of resources, the distribution of incomes, and the conditions under which food is produced and traded."[11] The root of the food problem in Colombia is not merely a serious imbalance in resource availability but an even more serious imbalance in the distribution of power and wealth among those who cultivate the land. The province of Garcia Rovira mirrors in almost a classic fashion the nature of these major constraints. In 1972 Garcia Rovira was chosen for "integrated rural development."[12] This province is typical of Colombia's Andean region; it has some public sector service institutions, and the majority of small farms in its agricultural sector makes it a microcosm of the problems and possibilities of rural underdevelopment.

Garcia Rovira is located in northeast Colombia. Its 295,700 hectares of mountainous land are largely unsuitable for agriculture, yet rapid population growth is increasingly forcing more marginal land into production. So far 25 percent of Garcia Rovira's land supports the cultivation of wheat, corn, potatoes, sugar cane, tobacco, and tomatoes. This land is cultivated so intensely and is so overgrazed that it has fallen victim to incessant erosion. More than half of the farmers use oxen and metal-tipped wooden plows for the preparation of their fields. With few communication and marketing facilities, with practically nonexistent electrification and controlled water supplies, and in the context of high population density and high illiteracy, it is not surprising that a majority of the 75 percent rural people of Garcia Rovira are not satisfied with their level of living. They simply do not want their children to become farmers.

Ninety-three and six-tenths percent of the farms of Garcia Rovira are less than 50 hectares in size; 70.1 percent are less than ten hectares, and 32.7 percent are less than four hectares. Large landowners with holdings of over 50 hectares in size control 6.4 percent of the farm units but in agricultural land those units represent 52.7 percent of the total area available for cultivation. Meanwhile farms of less than ten hectares in size cover 18.9 percent of the rural land. And more than 50 percent of the land owned by those farmers with holdings of less than four hectares is good for neither crop nor livestock production.

As of 1972 the farmers of Garcia Rovira were aware of the existence of better agricultural technologies. Biological technologies were used by at least 22 percent of the farmers, especially those concerned with tobacco, corn, and potatoes. But, in general, the use of new technologies and production inputs was still the luxury of a few cash crop farmers. It need not be surprising then that crop yields in Garcia Rovira are extremely low even by national standards. About 83 percent of the rural families of this province are poor. The above findings indicate

that rural poverty (and at the opposite end of the spectrum—rural wealth) is a direct reflection of the maldistribution of productive land, a lower level of education, tenancy (in which land ownership predominates in the high income strata), and a dual structure of production (in which a high proportion of the resources suitable to the low income farms is dedicated to corn, bean, pea, wheat and poultry production, in contrast with a greater percentage allocated to tobacco, potato, and dairy activities within the farms with higher income levels). Moreover, as expected, expenses for biological inputs are consistently higher within the high income farm group which allows them to reap greater harvests from production. For the most part, the rural poor are epitomized by an inadequate supply of productive land and capital, and a marginalization from the services that should provide them with needed resources for increased production, i.e., credit, improved inputs and education. Accordingly, "integrated rural development," to be more than a palliative, must face those variables characterizing rural poor (the size of the family, education, land tenure, stock of factors of production, the use of profit-increasing innovations), than to focus solely on creating changes in product mix on farms.[13]

THE "WHITE ELEPHANT," THE "DOCTORES," AND THE SMALL FARMER

Talk of land reform in Colombia is as dead an issue as the "integrated rural development projects" themselves. Visiting the headquarters of the Colombian Agricultural Institute (ICA) in Bogotá, one has the impression that the well-dressed bureaucracy is indeed working to solve the technical and social problems of agricultural technology transfer, the chief mission of ICA. But whether one talks to an administrator or a scientist of the Colombian agricultural elite, it soon becomes clear that a stultifying and bankrupt element dominates the vision even of those few who dare to be honest about the severe constraints within which they operate. Charts, projections, statistics of what is expected from current projects or future plans dominate the thinking of a largely American-trained agricultural elite. Knowing as it does that land reform, if and when it becomes a priority, certainly will *not* be one in the near future, this elite and the supporting foreign technical assistance experts try in vain to convince themselves that marginal technical assistance will keep them and the peasants out of trouble.

ICA in its present institutional structure dates back to 1963. As a young national institution it has great potential for growth and excellence. But the problems it faces are so numerous that ICA shows signs of old age. Its director, Rafael Mariño Navas, is an electrical engineer. And with more than 1000 professionals at its command, ICA has the image of the "white elephant" in Colombia. But this "white elephant" is not only urban and weak but he is chained to a complex web of constraints.

With its national headquarters in Bogotá, ICA enjoys administrative convenience in running its few regional offices and some 30 experiment stations, and has access to those making policies for agriculture. In Bogotá ICA has also developed a master's level graduate program in agricultural sciences. In 1967 the teaching of agricultural economics was added to the infant ICA graduate school. Two years later an American advisor assessed the training potential as well as the problems of agricultural economics at ICA this way:

> A general lack of understanding, some misunderstanding and little agreement prevails at high administrative levels in ICA about the role and functions of an Agricultural Economics Department. The inability of most technicians and professionals with specialized training to view the development problem as a whole is a common failing. The interdependence of commodity, production, marketing, and policy research and development programs is neither understood nor considered . . . . ICA has the best base for training agriculturalists in Colombia. The ultimate success in agricultural development in Colombia will not be measured in new or improved commodities at high rates of output but in the number and quality of trained agriculturalists to work with the agricultural sector in production and distribution.[14]

Apparently the advice of this American scientist fell on deaf ears. ICA's policies have focused on the development of "improved commodities" for the benefit of the rural elite. A scientist from the private agricultural sector put ICA's misdirected development policies in the context of the following critical constraints:

> New technologies ought to be directed toward the small farmer in Colombia. But ICA scientists do not really know the problems of the small farmer. Their research is usually of academic interest only. It is not designed to solve the problems of Colombian agriculture. It is necessary that ICA scientists go to the countryside and live with the farmers. The French experience in this direction can be paradigmatic to us. ICA can train medium level agricultural technicians to deal with the problems of the farmers. As it is the agronomic engineers of ICA never work in the rural sector. They go abroad for advanced studies and once back they take administrative positions. ICA scientists not only do not grow a crop for themselves but they do not know how to grow a crop. They are afraid to go to the farms. They speak other languages but Spanish.[15]

How do ICA scientists see ICA? They readily admit that theirs is not an enviable position. They lament the fact that nothing is done about land reform. They find some consolation that the government is trying to redistribute resources in the form of credit. They argue that the government is at least willing to spend money, that institutions do exist, and that ICA is in the process of initiating multidisciplinary social and economic research on the problems of the small farmer. But they also admit that such research and agrarian reform projects in the absence of sustained land reform are likely to raise peasant expectations and result in eventual rural trouble and violence.

The ICA technology and rural poverty predicament has also another dimension. An ICA regional director explained what he felt were the main problems in implementing "the tasks of rural development." This young ICA administrator and veterinarian served for two years in the city of Málaga, about nine hours by Jeep from Bogotá, in the province of Garcia Rovira—distinguished by a long tradition of rural poverty and violence. He said:

> Peasant traditionalism is hindering our efforts to improve the social and economic welfare of the small rural household. Peasant individualism is equally inimical to group work and cooperation in agricultural development. It is a fact that the nature of insufficient land resources, the prevalence of tiny land holdings, the poor quality of the soil and the systems of cultivation in existence demand appropriate work strategies in order to attain higher productivity, better production methods and increased income potential for all of the farmers of this region. Yet this province suffers from rapid population growth. Our integrated development programs are handicapped not merely by the existence of too many and large families but by the lack of resources, both economic and human. The infrastructure at our disposal is most inadequate for the needs of this area. This seriously affects production, marketing and the influence and transfer of technologies. We do not have the human and physical resources to match the size and population of the area we serve. Interinstitutional coordination needed for a serious and responsible team work and for better limited resource use has not been possible in the development of our programs. The conditions of this area demand that appropriate research and demonstration be carried out on the farmers' fields. The adoption of some of the traditional techniques may eventually lead to the development of appropriate technologies and strategies for their acceptance. It is the low economic conditions and the high cost and low availability of inputs that are essentially responsible for the slow adoption of technologies by the peasants of this region.[16]

ICA scientists who serve in regional offices and experiment stations have few if any library resources at their disposal. They receive low salaries and those are often behind payment schedule. Yet they enjoy considerable prestige in the small towns where they spend their brief absence from Bogotá. To the farmers they are the *doctores* who leave for the cities as quickly as they come, to dispense usually the wrong advice. Individual ICA scientists are certainly sincere men laboring under extremely adverse conditions. But ICA, like the foreign institutions operating in Colombia, is still trying to show that it is "good citizen" by refining the largely discredited trickle-down technology and knowledge transfer hypothesis.

FOREIGN INSTITUTIONS IN COLOMBIA: WILL THEIR STRATEGY OF FINANCIAL AND INTELLECTUAL PATERNALISM WORK?

While the Ford Foundation, for instance, sympathizes with the plight of the vast peasant (*campesino*) Colombian majority, its officers in Bogotá believe that without land reform there is not much anybody can do to put substance into the new Colombian elite's pride in "integrated rural development." However, the Ford Foundation in Colombia works within the existing social structure. It heavily supports ICA. Its main goal is that a lengthy investment in carefully selected members of the Colombian elite will eventually become the catalyst for appropriate changes in Colombian life and political economy. Only time will tell whether such a strategy of financial and intellectual paternalism will work or will be counterproductive. And time for Colombia and the foreign institutions it hosts is running out. If Colombia is to avoid another period of social violence it must destroy the fear that pervades all questions and priorities on rural development.

AN "ASSOCIATION FINANCED BY BIG CAPITALISTS"

Like all Colombian institutions, the International Center for Tropical Agriculture (CIAT), despite its international nature, operates within the Colombian context of fear and neglect of the small farmer. Located on a 522 hectare farm in the prosperous Valle del Cauca near the city of Cali, distinguished for the beauty of its women, CIAT enjoys the luxury of isolation from the real problems of tropical agriculture and especially those of Colombia. The six year old international center is housed in architecturally beautiful structures that combine Spanish elegance with modern convenience, expensively furnished, and operated with the support of all the labor-saving and capital-intensive technologies. Its experimental plots reflect agricultural technologies and production inputs that are for the most part beyond the reach of the small farmer.

Beyond this veneer of expensive technologies, CIAT does not have much to offer to Colombian or international tropical agricultural development. Its rice technologies "have reached very few small farmers." Its beef and bean programs have had no impact yet, and while the cassava technology has brought "spectacular results" in the controlled experimental plots, it still has to be transferred to the agricultural sector. The promising swine nutrition technology is slowly being dismantled and the small farmer project was recently abolished.

CIAT's short-lived small farmer project was apparently designed to work with the Colombian Agricultural Institute (ICA) in order to transfer technologies to the small farmer. No scientist or administrator of CIAT is able or willing to offer a reasonably concrete explanation for the failure of this project. Some say that the small farmer project was abolished for the following reasons:

1. CIAT did not approve of this experiment. It was initiated through external pressures.
2. There was intense conflict among the various scientists working on the project. The interest in some of those scientists was simply to create mathematical models in order to test their hypotheses on rural development.
3. A former leading administrator of CIAT was opposed to the small farmer project from the beginning. He never understood the strategy of small farmer development and had precious little interest in it.
4. The team of scientists could not agree on a definition of "the small farmer."
5. The director of the project "lost his objectivity" and did not even manage to get his staff together. Each member of the team worked alone.

In general, CIAT scientists agreed that the small farmer project was ill-conceived and ill-executed.

But there is another dimension to the failure of the small farmer project that transcends personal or institutional antagonisms developed within CIAT toward the small farmer. CIAT and the rest of the international agricultural research centers function in the context of a reward-penalty system. This means that the main raison d'être of these institutes is to increase the national yields of their commodity crops. To fail to do so is to lose their financial support. The implications of this technology transfer policy is that the centers have become "factories for producing technologies without any regard for the small farmer." It is easy to see then why from the very beginning CIAT as an institution said to those working on the small farmer project: "To hell with it." Moreover, some members of the small farmer CIAT team were talking as if their impact would have radical social consequences in the rural communities where they were working. This frightened the CIAT board of trustees and the small farmer project was abolished. The Colombian rural environment of unrest and gross social inequalities was certainly uncongenial for an international center to show what the transfer of technology could do to the low levels of living of the rural poor. CIAT and its sister institutions are "very sensitive to local political leadership." They claim they cannot work with peasant masses since that is the function of the national research centers. It is also argued that to transfer technology to the small farmer is to interfere with local affairs.[17] This position never has been sound. The international centers have transferred technologies to the big farmers and this has not caused friction with national leadership. What seems to be at stake, rather, is the unwillingness of these centers to develop the difficult technologies needed to cope and perhaps change the complex biological and social environment of the small farmer. Certainly the social position of the poor farmer is not likely to remain unchanged if he has at his disposal better technologies to improve his standards of living. It is this fear of change, transmitted as it is from the local elites, that either paralyzes the few socially concerned scientists of the international centers, or simply strengthens the monoculture commodity approach that transcends moral and social issues, adding an attractive, simplistic, but, in the long run, dangerous, strategy for "agricultural development" that still guides the international institutes.

A Colombian intellectual in Bogotá said that "CIAT is foreign to Colombia because as a research center it is highly divorced from Colombian problems. It has developed no small farmer technology, and its main emphasis is on high-yielding technologies for tropical agriculture." And an eighteen year old malnourished young man, son of a one and a half hectare farmer, living in a village about 75 kilometers from CIAT, defined the International Center for Tropical Agriculture as "an association financed by big capitalists." What makes this young man's definition of CIAT interesting is that it says something about the international institute. The great majority of the small farmers living 50 kilometers or more away from CIAT had not even heard of the institute. And certainly what this poor boy understood CIAT to be is complementary to the Bogotá intellectual's critical attitude toward the international research center. These two Colombian views of CIAT bring into sharp focus its precarious isolation in Colombian society.

And the luxurious investment in resources that CIAT makes for its non-Colombian senior scientists is another dimension of inequality that is highly resented in Colombia.

Some senior scientists at CIAT do not ask critical questions. All too often they do not take questions of social significance seriously. They take their fabulous material rewards for granted. They are critical of their United States colleagues for refusing to contribute to international agricultural research. They are equally critical of their Colombian colleagues for their failure to either generate or transfer technologies to the farmer. But it is the question of the small farmer that sharply divides the scientific establishment of CIAT. All agree that CIAT has not transferred any technologies to the small farmer. A CIAT senior scientist responsible for the new rice technology that benefited almost exclusively the rich farmers of Colombia sees the small farmer and the food problem of Colombia in terms of productivity alone. He subtly if instinctively separates his personal from his professional ethics for the implications of technology transfer. He sees the rapid disappearance of the small upland rice producer and outwardly he appears to be neither disturbed nor critically concerned with such a tragedy. His is a paradigm of technological development forcibly divorced from its social and institutional roots. How this scientist sees the uses of technology reflects the uncertain and increasingly dangerous technology transfer philosophy of CIAT and its sister institutions. He puts this issue in the following context:

> The small farmers in Colombia are causing great deforestation. They must be moved to the alluvial plains where some 40 to 50 million hectares of prime quality land, with plentiful if uncontrolled water supplies, still remain to be formally occupied. These plains provide the only alternative to the small upland rice producers. And yet the Colombian government does not know how to move these peasants to the plains. Both the irrigation and rice technologies for these plains must be designed on the Asian model. Rice is not comparable to other foodcrops because of the critical role of water to its sustenance. Scientists in the long run do not worry about the small farmers. They could be exploited but that is doubtful.[18]

Ideally this scientist's alluvial plains–small rice farmer model could work. But with the possible exception of China neither Colombia nor any other country has ever provided the ideal setting for the small farmer to flourish. What is disturbing about his proposal is not merely his total disregard for the fate of the thousands of small rice farmers who are indeed exploited and rapidly forced out of agriculture, but also his scientific, cold detachment from the crushing problems of rural poverty in Colombia.

DIET OF RICE, BANANAS, AND BONE SOUP

Nobody is more qualified to describe the conditions of rural poverty in Colombia than the poor farmer himself. Not far from CIAT a black farmer, who must support 11 children on less than one hectare, put the social and technological dimensions of rural poverty in their proper if bleak perspective:

> I am 60 years old but I have never managed to escape the crushing weight of poverty. Every day I work from six in the morning to six in the evening. On my land I grow cassava, coffee and bananas. Despite the high price of coffee, my income from this crop is very low because most of the profits are made by intermediaries. I supplement my coffee income by selling wood. My daily concern is for food and clothing for my family. Rice, bananas, and bone soup make our daily diet. I need more land. I need some technical assistance but no agronomist has ever helped me. I do not know what CIAT is. But I know what the Colombian Agricultural Institute (ICA) is. Yet I would not ask for ICA's advice. I know of a farmer who was wiped out because he accepted the suggestions of the ICA agronomists. ICA lends money with interest that is even higher than that charged by the Agrarian Bank.[19] Needless to say I have never managed to get credit from anybody. I deal with the grocer on a barter basis. It has not been easy to survive in this area. In 1937 there were enough small farmers all around me. Now their farms are pasture land for the big landlords while the original owners have become serf workers for about 35 pesos per day. In the 1940s rich farmers sprayed the small farmers' crops with poison or frequently flooded our plots in order to force us to run away. Today when the government tries to help us, for instance to give us inexpensive implements, these efforts usually fail because of the resistance of the local rural elite. There is an intense fear that pervades the life of the small farmer. He cannot fish, hunt, or cut his trees. The big fish eats the small one.[20]

Not merely fear but uncertainty cripples all the efforts of the sharecropper to raise his levels of living. At the ICA experiment station El Arsenal in the small village Enciso in the province of Garcia Rovira, seven men and one woman ranging in age from the early twenties to the late fifties shared with me their emotional reflections on their predicament as sharecroppers. Their former landlord was a tobacco company. Their present landlord is ICA. With assured technical knowledge on tobacco, which these small farmers cultivate on plots no larger than two hectares, the greatest constraints to their aspiration for a better standard of living appeared to be their insecurity of tenure and the small size of their land. In the presence of several agricultural scientists from ICA it was not surprising that these sharecroppers, who at present "volunteer" their labor to the ICA experiment station, would direct their remarks to past developments. Their former landlord, the tobacco company, was the obvious, if not the only, target of their anger:

> We own neither a house nor a farm. Each one of us has a single room for a house, without electricity or easy availability of water. Our boys attend no more than the first five years of the elementary school. They also start working at the farm at the age of five. Our young people leave the farms and migrate to Venezuela or try to find a job in the cities. Our main problem is the low profitability of the tobacco we produce with great labor. It is necessary to take good care of all kinds of crops today. We would like to grow foodcrops but it is very difficult to get credit for their cultivation. Corn is very susceptible to insect attacks and cannot be stored. With tobacco we manage the risk. And at least tobacco gives us ready access to cash. Even for tobacco cultivation the price of the inputs is increasing at a faster rate than the price of the final product we sell. Our condition today is worse than some years ago. It is the middle man who classifies our agricultural produce, even if it is of the same quality, fixes the prices we receive and cheats us blind. There is no way to complain for our problems since the owner of the land is never here. The landlord also decides on the crop the sharecropper has to grow. We know of some regions where the landlords give their workers *ayo*, leaves that contain cocaine. In this way the workers neither feel hungry nor get easily tired. In return the owners of the land receive labor that is both productive and inexpensive.[21]

The village priest in Colombia is also a landlord. Perhaps more than the lay landlord, the ecclesiastical landlord keeps the medieval traditions of serfdom intact. In a small village near the city of Málaga in the province of Garcia Rovira a woman in her fifties described what it meant to be materially dependent on the village priest. Living as she does in a dark, small, one room mud hut without even a garden to grow vegetables this woman shares her prehistoric housing amenities with her 85 year old father, her brother, his wife, and two children of nine and five years old. Her "house" is on the 50 hectare farm of the village priest. But the priest saw it wise to put a wire fence around the little hut lest its occupants be tempted to grow some corn. For ten years this family has managed to survive in this environment that is neither human nor fit for human habitation. Admitting as she did that the members of her family were *cuidanderos,* or serfs, this woman continued:

This 50 hectare farm does not really belong to the priest. It belongs to the Holy Virgin. My father still earns our main income. He is the grave digger for the village. The priest pays my father 20 pesos a month[22] for his job. Sometimes relatives of those buried also give some money to my father. Once my sister-in-law asked the priest for help in order to enroll her nine year old son in the local elementary school but the priest said he was too poor to be able to assist others. Meanwhile our priest owns the local radio station and the public swimming pool. He has organized what he calls "the chicken day" when all farmers must give a chicken to the church.[23]

VICTIMS OF EXPLOITATION AND MALNUTRITION

It is disturbing to have witnessed, as I did in rural Colombia, the most gross inequalities that the beast in man has made possible. The conditions of extreme rural poverty can be described at a loss of sensitivity to the human condition. The rural poor in Colombia have large families, and very small and unfertile farms; they lack capital, technology, and the necessary inputs; and they are victims of exploitation and malnutrition. Their children have few of the social amenities that the rest of the young enjoy. With the virtual absence of educational resources the rural young either stay in the rural sector, destined to inherit an even smaller piece of land, become agricultural workers for a nonliving wage at the age of six to ten; or migrate to the cities, where jobs are increasingly hard to find.

The small peasant farmer is proud of his accomplishment. He has survived a harsh biological and social environment. Through centuries of experience, his is still the best agricultural technology for producing food in balance with nature. Modern agricultural research can solve the food problem only by utilizing the knowledge that the farmer possesses. But the small Colombian farmer is also angry. He resents his rich rural neighbor. He equally resents the presence of armed soldiers in his tiny village. He resists the efforts of the rural elite that are slowly pushing him out of his tiny farm, depriving him not merely of the only profession he has mastered, but in effect destroying his way of life. From 1960 to 1970, 90,298 farms of less than five hectares were simply eliminated in Colombia (Tables 3–1 and 3–2). Knowing as we do that each small farm supports at least ten people it becomes clear that close to one million rural people in just the decade of the sixties were

Table 3–1. Farms in Colombia by Size Group, 1960

Size Group	Number of Farms	Area in Hectares
Less than 5 hectares	756,605	1,238,976
From 5 to 20 hectares	238,376	2,736,825
From 20 to 100 hectares	126,779	5,319,172
More than 100 hectares	42,913	18,044,854
Total	1,209,672	27,337,827

Source: Pierre Gilhodès, "Agrarian Struggles in Colombia," in *Agrarian Problems and Peasant Movements in Latin America,* edited by Rodolfo Stavenhagen (New York: Anchor Books, 1970), p. 450, Table 2.

forced to migrate to the cities and/or to become agricultural workers. At about the same time the mechanization of Colombian agriculture reached its climax. In 1950 there were about 6500 tractors in Colombia. By 1973 the tractor population had increased to 23,800 units.[24]

THE PREDICAMENT OF THE RURAL POOR: POWERLESS AND ISOLATED

The small farmer feels powerless. There is a certain fatalism in his attitude toward life and his predicament of poverty. He asks for more land, better technologies, and better prices for his produce; and he wants credit. He is friendly and hospitable to foreigners and if treated with appropriate consideration the poor farmer describes the origins, evolution, and nature of rural poverty with a precision and a passion that stagger the emotions and imagination of the observer. The poor farmer has a long memory. In Colombia he remembers the days of violence when his rich neighbor poisoned his crops in order to force him to abandon his land. He remembers the days when the sugarcane producers charged him dear prices for water to irrigate his crops—a function that either continues or has been taken over by public corporations. He mistrusts some of his fellow small farmers and the rest of the social order. Even when land becomes available through land reform, the small farmer is not likely to accept it without serious hesitation. Neither does he seek the advice of the agricultural scientist. The small farmer in Colombia "does not want to bother the technician."

It is not surprising that the poor Colombian peasant farmer does not have much trust in the agricultural technical assistance elite of his country. The small farmer knows that the number of those who grow food is continuously decreasing. He is keenly aware that the day may be approaching when he will be pushed out of agriculture. Meanwhile "the food situation in Colombia is dramatically deteriorating. And the distribution of land is showing pathological consequences. Peasants

Table 3-2.   Farms in Colombia by Size Group, 1960 and 1970 (Rapid Disappearance of the Small Farmer)

Size Group in Hectares	Number of Farms				Area in Thousands of Hectares			
	1960		1970		1960		1970	
	Number	*Percent*	*Number*	*Percent*	*Hectares*	*Percent*	*Hectares*	*Percent*
Less than 1	298,071	24.7	251,262	22.1	132	0.5	119.5	0.4
From 1 to less than 3	308,352	25.5	278,555	24.4	546	2.0	484.2	1.5
From 3 to less than 5	150,182	12.4	136,490	12.0	561	2.0	505.8	1.6
From 5 to less than 10	169,145	14.0	155,547	13.7	1,165	4.3	1,067.2	3.4
From 10 to less than 50	201,020	16.6	217,236	19.0	4,211	15.4	4,685.7	15.0
From 50 to less than 100	39,990	3.3	48,788	4.3	2,680	9.8	3,267.1	10.4
From 100 to less than 500	36,010	3.0	43,415	3.8	6,990	25.6	8,420.8	26.9
From 500 to less than 1000	4,141	0.3	4,887	0.4	2,771	10.0	3,229.7	10.2
From 1000 and over	2,761	0.2	3,332	0.3	8,322	30.4	9,598.7	30.6
Total	1,209,672	100.0	1,139,502	100.0	27,338	100.0	31,378.7	100.0

Source: Juan Enrique Araya et al., *La política agraria en Colombia 1950–1975* (Bogotá: Fundacion para la Education Superior y el Desarrollo, 1975), p. 8.

are invading land and they themselves are being invaded by other peasants."[25]

THE BANKRUPTCY OF LAND REFORM

In this context the rural elite that rules Colombia cannot afford to let the issue of land reform die, but neither is it willing to permit the Colombian institute for agrarian reform (INCORA) to function. IN-CORA has been losing even the limited resources put at its disposal when it was founded in 1961. The work of this land reform institute has become even more problematic and complex with the new 1975 legislation that limits its ability to buy unproductive land owned by big landlords. It takes five years for INCORA to distribute a piece of land to landless peasants. In 1974 INCORA had the following technical assistance talent:[26]

Agronomic Engineers	204
Veterinarians	74
Animal Technicians	8
Forest Engineers	9
Agricultural Engineers	1
Agronomists	4
Agricultural Economists	4
Credit and Extension Workers	545
Total	849

As if these legal and technological constraints were not sufficiently binding, INCORA has been subjected to severe criticism and has in effect been divorced from the question of land reform. And to make certain that this land reform institute will abandon its main legal function altogether, the Colombian ruling elite is presently dividing INCORA into two equally ineffectual entities.

It hardly needs to be said that this intellectually restrictive and morally bankrupt environment is congenial neither to the few socially concerned agricultural scientists nor to technology generation and transfer. Some members of the Colombian scientific elite look to Cuba and China for inspiration. Others simply keep themselves in the big cities and away from the grim rural realities of their country. They realize that the question of the small farmer must be addressed immediately, but they are afraid to transcend theory to action. They even realize that their own attitudes and social distance from the poor farmer are major constraints but are incapable of bridging the gap of their own ignorance. They are prisoners not merely of an agricultural education that is largely theoretical and divorced from reality, but even more fundamentally they are and continue to be prisoners of advanced training in the temperate zone's scientific, economic, and agricultural schools. It need not be surprising that very little agricultural technology generation and transfer takes place in Colombia. With the social and institutional avenues of technology transfer essentially closed, what technology reaches the field of the small farmer is usually wrong and causes more damage and social dislocation than increased food production and better levels of living. It is no wonder then that the small farmer is not willing "to bother the technician."

Colombia's Predicament with Technology, Rural Poverty, and Rural Violence: Redressing the Imbalance Between Man and Land

TECHNOCRATIC STRATEGY OF AGRICULTURAL MODERNIZATION

Guided as it has been by rich country development specialists, Colombia has followed a technocratic strategy of agricultural modernization. The single economic goal of increasing the output of the agricultural sector necessitates that either more land is brought under the plow or that better technologies replace traditional farming practices. The political economy of the technocratic strategy of agricultural development allows competition, private property, and the mechanism of the free market to be the main context within which higher agricultural output is supposed to be reached. There is nothing wrong with the higher output objective of this strategy. In fact it is absolutely essential that Colombia and other poor countries do raise their food production. What is wrong with the technocratic agricultural strategy is the fact that it is devoid of social responsibility. Private property, land, and the benefits of new technologies, reflected as they are in the gross inequalities of the existing land tenure systems, are at the command of a small landowning elite. The concentration of wealth at the hands of the few not only penalizes the many, but in no way does it guarantee that the agricultural output will be increased.

In Colombia a good proportion of the labor force is tied up in producing just enough food for local consumption. The high man-land ratio and the extremely low yields per acre result in disastrously low real incomes for most of the rural people. In addition to strengthening existing social inequalities, this low productivity certainly perpetuates the serious nutritional deficiencies of the poor. Considering that undernutrition and/or malnutrition exist in the context of infectious and parasitical diseases, bad housing facilities, and a low level of public and private hygiene and sanitation, then the nutrition factor critically determines and reflects the interdependence of the technological and social dimensions of development.

If, in Colombia, poverty and low yields cause low nutritional levels, appropriate advanced technologies in an appropriate land tenure context can correct the imbalances of subsistence agriculture, supported as it is by the underutilization of the huge rural labor force. New technologies need not be labor saving. In fact they require a higher and more efficient input of labor. Technological reforms and improvements demand more work in preparing the soil, sowing, weeding, and harvesting. Controlled water supplies also depend on labor utilization in the construction as well as the preservation of the irrigation works.

IRRIGATION MANAGEMENT INSTITUTIONS

It is a fact that controlled water supplies have always helped farmers increase the productivity of their land. In this context it is not surprising that irrigation has been a critical factor in the new Colombian-developed agricultural technologies. Despite the rapid increase in the availability of irrigation water, the irrigation management institutions of Colombia impede rather than facilitate the productive use of controlled water supplies. The small peasant farmer for the most part is left without irrigation water; or he has to pay a dear price which he usually cannot afford. Irrigation water in Colombia is at the command of government corporations or serves the needs of the landed elite. The Colombian Agricultural Institute developed better technologies only for irrigated crops and farms of the landowning elite. But even with its rural elite monopoly, the amount of water that does reach the land has little relationship to its efficient use or the social cost of its productivity. This mismanagement of water resources reflects the technical as well as the social distance from the realities of agriculture of those who either manage or own irrigated water. But the inefficiencies of controlled water supplies in Colombia mirror also the institutionalized rigidities of the existing irrigation management institutions. Controlled water supplies are a weapon, both financial and social, at the hands of the rural elite in order to control the small farmer. The big landlord sells his water; but he can also interrupt the water supply to the small farmer at critical periods, or simply flood his land at will.

RESOURCE ALLOCATION AND TECHNOLOGY

In Colombia the single, most negative constraint to agricultural development is the failure of the landowning elite to allow agrarian reforms to correct the abysmal inequalities that govern the life of the rural majority. It need not be overemphasized that sharecropping undermines technology transfer and its sustained and efficient utilization. Sharecropping is also inimical to resource allocation for the very advances in agricultural technology that alone can raise labor utilization and yields. In Colombia most of the rural people have no surplus income or even enough land to permit a reasonable increase in agricultural investment. But those who own most of the rural income and land have shown no interest in bettering their farms and raising their productivity. Perhaps they do not have the capacity to commit themselves seriously to farming. Instead, the Colombian landowning elite spends its profits on luxury consumption or on urban investment, or simply sends them out of the country. Even a recently passed tax of 8 percent on the expected productivity of land is generating a storm of protest among the members of the rural Colombian elite. In effect, the large estate owners are telling the government that if this new law is enforced they will simply speed up the rate with which they export their earnings from the agricultural sector.

In the context of gross and increasing inequality in the agricultural sector of Colombia, an agricultural revolution like that intended by CIAT and fueled only by technology will create grave problems that will threaten the very fabric of development and civilization in vast regions of that country. *It is now necessary that the governing elite of Colombia bring its rural majority into the realm of political power and technology.* This means that land reforms ought to redress the imbalance between land and man so that the poor peasant can have the opportunity to use existing technologies for food production and for exercising an active role in the political economy of his society. This also means that the rich countries can no longer offer technical assistance to the rich-country-educated Colombian elite without first considering the social implications of technical knowledge. The governments of the developed countries must be willing to design their appropriate technologies to benefit the small peasant farmer. And they must also be willing to see that their technical assistance *does reach* the small

Colombian farmer. *It appears, then, that land reform, bringing as it does social and economic justice and contributing to higher productivity, is a critical development priority for Colombia.*

DUAL SOCIETIES

Facts dictate that the elites of the rich and of the poor countries must direct their technological resources to the solution of the global poverty problem. Yet the past record of such a development is bleak:

> The oligarchies, the elites, and their clients, who represent an infinitesimally small percentage of the people in the underdeveloped world, have managed so far to quell disorder and retard social change. They continue to control the social sources of what men think and how they perform. Their activities unfold not on the land they so guardedly hold but at the power stations of their nation's universities, industries, embassies, ministries, and many times in the halls of the United Nations. They, and their generally less landed but far more influential counterparts in the advanced countries, who frequent similar places, are the incarnation of the social impasse. On their desks the real problems of the poor, economic and social development, and the green revolution converge, and go no further.[1]

It is only the nature of the food problem and of technology that have the potential to convince the various elites that self-interest alone demands that the poor be brought into the realm of a better level of living. In the last three years no economic disorder has appeared "more certain than the disorder in food. It does not pass. It has little to do with changes in the weather. It is a sign of lasting insecurity in the world food economy. It is political and economic, and it could have been avoided."[2] Technology is certainly no disorder. Yet mismanaged technology becomes not merely a lasting disorder but it strengthens the institutionalization of a dual society of gross inequalities. An Indian scientist explained the relationship of technology and the dual society of India. But what he says about India certainly fits the context of Colombian development:

> Technology is like genetic material. It carries the code of the society in which it was born and sustained, and tries to reproduce that society . . . its structure, its social values. The adoption of a capital-intensive, luxury-oriented western technology in India has thus created a dual society—metropolitan centres of western-oriented affluence amidst vast expanses of rural poverty, mass unemployment, large migrations to cities and wide income disparities. Even the talk about technological self-reliance today implies the indigenous development of the western

brand of technology. This will only preserve, and strengthen, the dual society. What is needed is a basically different pattern of technology suited to our conditions and needs.[3]

Appropriate social and economic development in India, Colombia, and other poor countries must give top priority to the development of *technologies of inequality reduction*. For instance:

(i) capital-saving and employment-generating rather than capital-intensive and labour-saving technologies; (ii) cottagescale and smallscale rather than largescale technologies; (iii) technologies appropriate to produce goods for mass consumption rather than for individual luxuries; (iv) technologies requiring little skill or small modifications in the skills of traditional craftsmen like potters, weavers, blacksmiths, carpenters, cobblers, tanners and oil millers; (v) technologies using local materials, rather than materials which have to be imported or transported from distant parts of the country; (vi) energy-saving rather than energy-intensive technologies; (vii) locally available sources of energy such as the sun, wind, and nightsoil and manure gas; (viii) machine tool industry for the technology of mass-producing, scaled-down, dispersible, miniaturised factories; (ix) technologies of *manu*-facture rather than *machino*-facture; and (x) technologies which promote a symbiotic and mutually reinforcing, rather than parasitic and destructive, dependence of metropolitan industry upon the rural population.[4]

THE SMALL FARMER CHALLENGE

An enormous increase in agricultural productivity even without new technologies is very much possible in Colombia. But it is necessary to repeat that such a possibility can materialize only in the context of sustained and innovative social reform. This means that the Colombian government must destroy the fear and contempt that the small farmer inspires in the country's ruling elites. Aside from ordering the army back to its barracks and out of the small farmer's backyard, a first step in bridging the gap between the dual society in Colombia would be to provide more land, make credit available, and take other steps to insure that the tremendous social and productivity potentials of the small farmer find a congenial environment to grow.

It is pertinent here to point out that it will not be easy to convince the urban and rural elite that the agrarian reform institute (INCORA) must be strengthened rather than dismantled. After all, the existing land tenure structure provides for cheap labor, cheap food, and fabulous returns for luxury consumption. But this elite must also be aware that the same land tenure system is slowly eroding the ecological as well as the human environment of Colombia. It is pointless to hold tenaciously to a largely undermined colonial legacy of keeping the majority of the population in a state of perpetual poverty and malnutrition. If not human kindness, at least technology and energy have made slavery obsolete. And since Colombia is not likely to turn her technological clock backward, it is reasonable to assume that enough members of the elite will have the courage to face the fundamental fact that the small farmers, constituting as they do the most productive sector of Colombian society, deserve more land, technical assistance, and credit.

The Colombian elite is not a monolithic social class of privilege and power. The president of Colombia, Alfonso López Michelsen, is very much aware of and sensitive to the problems and potentials of the small farmer. Around 1960 he founded the Revolutionary Liberal Movement (*Movimiento Revolucionario Liberal,* or MRL) in an attempt to channel the revolutionary implications of rural violence into political action and reform. From its inception MRL received its electoral support from the rural sector. And whatever the meaning of the current state of siege and of the policies of "integrated rural development," it is becoming increasingly clear to the Colombian elite that the peasant today has changed. *He demands more than a subsistence wage.* And President López Michelsen and other members of the elite know they cannot possibly turn their backs on the just demands of the peasant. Colombia has also changed. Less than half of the population lives in the countryside. A great deal of the land remains partially or totally uncultivated. Meanwhile, the contradiction between the more than a million landless peons and the 8000 who own about 70 percent of the land will continue to feed the sparks of a violent revolution unless land reform and technologies of inequality reduction defuse the precarious if temporary silence in the rural society of Colombia.

An equally explosive contradiction is inherent in the agricultural commodities price policies and consumption taxes that force the rural poor to make a substantial contribution to industrial development. Some members of the Colombian elite are aware that modernization of their country demands the elimination of backwardness and of its supporting modern economic and rural feudal institutions as much as the peasant does. Two representatives of the powerful private agricultural sector saw development in the following context:

> Politics is keeping Colombia backward. The land reform institute took land from the "good farmers" and gave it to the small farmers who did not know how to farm. Productive land ought to stay where it is. It should not be redistributed. Political and social issues dominated land

reform but not economic concerns. For instance, those small farmers who received land through the actions of the land reform institute were burdened by high prices for at least ten years in order to pay for their acquired farms. Rapid population growth is our number one problem. The state is working timidly on family planning. And education is the critical issue in this question. The parish priest is more conservative than the official church hierarchy. No doubt the church will lose its campaign against family planning. Everybody is crazy making money. The whole question of development has to be rethought. The problems of ecology and pollution cannot be ignored for long. Progress must be considered in the context of raising the human condition. The social system of Colombia ought to be dismantled. Our inspirations must be guided by past experience. A balance between the city and the countryside is a necessary step to development. This means that in our efforts to lessen inequalities we must deemphasize material values while at the same time we emphasize spiritual values. Certainly if technology is introduced in an inequal social structure it strengthens that inequality.[5]

Credit, like technology, follows the same social law. In Colombia there is a positive relationship between the indebtedness of the poor farmer or landless agricultural worker and the wealth of the landlords. It is also a fact that the very poor rural people cannot obtain credit. And the annual interest rate for those farmers who do get credit is extraordinarily high. It ranges from 36 percent to 60 percent depending on whether the lender is the Agrarian Bank or the local store owner. The productivity of the small farmer has demonstrated beyond any reasonable doubt that high returns for capital investment in the rural sector are feasible. *It is necessary then that the Colombian government assure the small farmer of markets, technical assistance, the availability of inputs, and credit at nominal interest rates.* The immediate result of such a policy would be the creation of employment in the agricultural sector, the generation of higher incomes for the rural people, the improvement of their daily diets, a substantial contribution to the national economy, and the stemming of the migration to the cities.

In such a new context, where the agricultural sector would occupy the top resource priority it deserves, the Colombian scientific elite would have no trouble generating better agricultural technologies for the diverse tropical ecological zones of the country. As it is, Colombia has perhaps the best and largest agricultural talent in Latin America. The International Center for Tropical Agriculture (CIAT) could help Colombia by abandoning its misused monoculture technologies and concentrating instead on the real problems of the small farmers. CIAT could also develop a Ph.D. program in tropical agricultural sciences on its beautiful campus. The board of trustees of CIAT and of the other international agricultural research centers must stop playing the unproductive game of pleasing the local elites. They ought to talk less about the "miracle" green revolution varieties and more about the small farmer and the elimination of rural poverty. And if a host country makes it impossible for an international center to reach the rural poor, then that center ought to close down.

It is outright criminal for the international community that supports these centers to waste precious scarce resources simply to strengthen the national elites. The U. S. Congress has a direct interest in this mismanagement and misallocation of resources. The 1973 and 1975 Foreign Assistance Acts directed the Agency for International Development (AID) to allocate its funds for the benefit of the poor majorities of the underdeveloped countries. AID is one of the contributing agencies to CIAT. And yet we have documented that CIAT and its technologies are completely unknown to the Colombian rural poor. Not only has CIAT failed to reach with its technologies the Colombian and Latin American tropical small farmer, but apparently it does not have any concrete policies to do so in the future. Unless CIAT does change its development and technology transfer strategies in the directions suggested in these pages, any further AID support would certainly be inappropriate and perhaps illegal in the context of the new U.S. law on foreign assistance.

A CIAT scientist raised the question as to "when" will CIAT be "discovered" by the leftist groups of Colombia. The question is not so much for the leftist Colombians as for the rural poor to discover CIAT. And until CIAT and its sister institutions do something for the rural poor theirs will be a precarious and dangerous position to maintain.

THE MULTINATIONAL CORPORATIONS, GLOBAL INTERDEPENDENCE, AND HUNGER

The multinational enterprise in Colombia has equally bypassed the poor. The small industrial city of Yumbo, just 11 kilometers from Cali in the Valle del Cauca, mirrors the kind of technological development that the Colombian technocrats, assisted by the multinational corporations, have forced on the country. Aside from the industrial goods produced at Yumbo, the city itself is rapidly becoming unfit for human habitation. With dangerously polluted drinking water resources, both controlled and uncontrolled, and heavily polluted air, those industrial workers who live in Yumbo cannot expect a long life. With decaying buildings and ugly corrosive slums, the town's spent humanity has all but given up. And yet the problem of industrial pollution in Yumbo has not caused much concern to either the development policymakers of Cali and Bogotá or to the chief executives of the multinational corporations responsible for the human and environmental damage to this small Colombian city. A Colombian scientist working for a U. S. company in Cali explained why Colombia does not have pollution control legislation:

> When a government official arrives from Bogotá to inspect an industrial plant at Yumbo he is taken by the corporation executives to the best Cali hotel where he is given dinner, offered a beautiful girl, and then returned to the airport to fly to Bogotá. The official never sees the industrial plant he came here to examine. Nevertheless, he signs all necessary documents and departs for his government office in Bogotá. He has no real choice in this affair. To refuse the entertainment and demand to inspect the plants will eventually result in the loss of his job. And when the government does ask the corporations to limit their pollution of the environment these companies threaten to leave Colombia.[6]

With this limited, perhaps biased, but nevertheless devastating evidence against the policies of some of the multinational corporations in Colombia, one fact is clear: The educated Colombian is becoming concerned with the impact of these companies on his country's development. No doubt not all corporations follow the same strategies. The issue of "social responsibility" is increasingly popular among multinational corporation executives. A chief executive of IBM said that in Colombia the company built a school. Moreover, IBM relies on the Colombian general manager of IBM Colombia to recommend where the company could start a socially responsible project.[7] The flow with this argument is that it hides more good intentions than good works. Besides, the local manager is a member of the urban, ruling elite who perhaps has never seen the rural poor and who would have little interest in their welfare. Most multinational corporation executives, like some scientists of the international agricultural research centers and other Western development specialists, find it interesting to talk about the rural poor and the global food problem. But they refuse to turn their theoretical and often humanitarian speculations into concrete action. Multinational company executives attend and finance conferences to justify their "social responsibility." And yet they are not willing even to encourage, much less support, research to explore ways for the corporations to help the poor farmer break the vicious chains of poverty. This does not mean that the multinational enterprise has suddenly lost its ability to transfer capital, technology, management, and skills to Colombia or any other country. Rather, this global institution shows evidence of ossification with decaying ideas and development priorities. It feels comfortable with elite-consumed technologies, elite-inspired economic thinking, and elite-controlled social and political structures. It does not feel comfortable with the only idea that will make or break its prized notion of "interdependence". Can there really be "global interdependence" in a meaningful sense when over a billion people go to bed hungry every day?

Colombia can become a paradigm to the other poor countries by forcing the more than 50 corporations operating within its borders to consider this question. It can accomplish this reordering of priorities by legislation that will make it mandatory for multinational enterprises to invest or grant a considerable proportion of their earnings to providing training, management, capital, technology, and other resources and services to the small farmer. And the institutions to facilitate and implement such a transfer of technological and material resources from the multinational enterprise to the small farmer not only exist in Colombia but welcome such challenging development possibilities.

SMALL FARMER PARTICIPATION TECHNOLOGIES

Perhaps the best way to invest any new resources in agricultural development would be to strengthen the existing experiment stations of the Colombian Agricultural Institute and/or create new research and development centers precisely in the areas where rural poverty is the rule rather than the exception. The philosophical foundation of each of these research and development centers ought to be based on the active participation and agricultural wisdom of the small farmer. This is not a theory that is suggested for purely idealized personal concerns. The fact is that the farmer is the best judge of what he does and what he hopes to do better. The farmer will improve his methods of production and accept new technologies only if he has been an active participant in the generation of the new technologies. This does not mean that each farmer be made a laboratory assistant, but rather that the scientist must have the common sense to involve the farmer in his work.

The direction of research is a critical factor in this development strategy. Agricultural research at these centers must seek to understand the nature and optimum conditions of the symbiotic cultivation of foodcrops, the use of plant residues for animal feed and energy, and the development of better, high risk-aversion technologies that will be fueled by manual labor. Small farm production is very complicated.

Agricultural research not only needs to generate technological knowledge. To reach sound policy decisions it must also seek to (1) describe and analyze current small farmer agricultural systems; (2) provide guidance for the organization of small farmer labor exchange and cooperative institutional arrangements for the sharing of inputs; (3) define the agricultural calendar for the cultivated crops; and (4) describe and analyze the small farmer's working, leisure, food, and nutrition patterns and habits.

The small farmers are no more homogeneous as a social class than the rural or urban elites. Access to land, water, capital, and technologies determine the composition of the local village power structure. The new agricultural research and development centers must avoid the temptation to become the tools of the village elites. They must provide equal opportunity for all the small farmers to use their inequality-reducing, labor-intensive, risk-aversion technologies and technical and social assistance and services. The goal of these centers will be facilitated if they also become the mechanism for the availability of credit and the instrument of land reform for the region they serve.

CAN AGRICULTURE IN COLOMBIA BECOME A MAGNET FOR RESOURCE GROWTH AND DEVELOPMENT? SOCIAL COST-BENEFIT ANALYSIS

If Colombia is to avoid further rural violence[8] on a large, disruptive scale, or the social collapse that its double population will likely bring in about 25 years, then it must now make its agriculture a magnet for resource growth and development, both human and material. The Colombian elites will pay a price for such a reordering of priorities. Some landlords will see the uncultivated portions of their huge estates confiscated and distributed to landless peasants. It will not be easy for the city professional class to buy and sell land for profit. Equally it will not be easy for the agricultural scientists to spend most of their time in Bogotá or Cali. But the price the Colombian elites have to pay for this fundamental change in their development policies is worth paying, since the returns, both intellectual and material, are high. In terms of intellectual benefit Colombia can easily become the capital of Latin America. Colombia then will export more than coffee. It will be able to export food, talent, and technology.

It would be silly to argue that these proposals are easy to implement, demand few resources, and simply satisfy the present ambitions of the Liberal ruling party. Certainly President López has a broad enough consensus to set the foundations for the long-range planning and investment necessary to understand and solve the critical problem of technology and rural poverty in Colombia.[9] But why has neither López nor his colleagues of the Colombian ruling elite done much for the rural poor? And why have the elites of the underdeveloped countries ignored the gross inequalities and equally gross rural poverty in their midst? Some say that this is an irrelevant question. They argue that since the elites have the wealth and the guns they simply do not care for the poor, be they in the city or in the countryside. And those who have been trained in economics explain poverty in terms of productivity. To accept these two propositions is to codify the law of the jungle, and to make it the iron law of history. But history has no iron law for those who study and learn from the past. The adult brown bear often kills its own kind, especially the powerless cubs. Man has also killed his fellow man. It would be absurd to conclude from this fact that man has always killed and always will be killing other men. Man has more than the beastly element in him. He has what is truly human in his virtue of philanthropy. He has also created music, art, literature, history, science, and technology to serve his intellectual and material welfare. It is obvious then that neither man nor history are easily dismissed by rigid, dogmatic, or superficial explanations of his behavior and action. Man and his actions are infinitely complex. Why the rural poor in Colombia have not fared any better is a complex question.

I went to Colombia to test my hypothesis on the critical nature of the social and institutional constraints in the transfer of agricultural science and technology to the poor countries. My experience in Colombia transformed my hypothesis into a thesis. Technology transfer is above all a human enterprise. The generation of better technologies is a critical component in increasing food production. But equally critical components are how these technologies are transferred, what are the needed inputs for the successful adoptation of the new knowledge, and who benefits from its availability. In Colombia rural poverty constitutes a major if not the only constraint in the absence of technologies from the small farm sector. No doubt the fact that the Colombian small farmer has not been touched by technology partially explains his low levels of living. But the roots of rural poverty, as this essay suggests, are imbedded not merely in the technological but in the social, institutional, religious, and political fabric of Colombian society. The Colombian elite and the elites of other underdeveloped countries can help their poor rural majorities attain higher standards of living. In Colombia this task will be easier to accomplish thanks to the politicization of the small farmer. Rural violence brought power to the peasant. It has made it easier for him to close the gap from the periphery to the center.

It has thrust him to the edge of political economy and polity. The transfer of agricultural science and technology to the small farmer will immensely facilitate this long, and, in the past, violent and infinitely slow transition. It will also provide a humane and sound way out of the predicament of unbalanced technological growth and rural poverty. The food problem will then recede into history.

Poverty-Stricken, Elite-Ridden Rural Economies: Institutional Structures and Unbalanced Technological Change

NEW TECHNOLOGIES AND THE POOR

Land tenure systems determine the prevailing patterns of rural income distribution as much in Colombia as in the rest of the poor countries. Traditional technologies leave their imprint on these patterns. For instance, the costs of indivisible inputs like bullocks have a greater impact on the livelihood of the small farmer than they do on the income of large landowners. The Bangladesh small peasant farmer rarely owns draft animals. He can share, hire, or exchange animal labor. This means that the income effect of the divisibility of this animal input on the small farmer reflects his land resources. Even more profoundly than traditional technologies, the new seed-fertilizer-water technologies are intimately interrelated with income distribution, and, above all, they depend on resource access and availability.

Bangladesh

It is pertinent here to document the above thesis even further. In 1960 Village Dhanishwar in East Bengal had the following resources: (1) 77 families or 426 persons; (2) 163 houses; (3) 41 plows, 8 plowing bulls, and 108 cows. Each family cultivated an average of 3.2 acres, if the 12 landless families are excluded. This village had no land for grazing and farming was the main occupation of 60 families. With few sharecroppers this village's land tenure was more equitable than in Bangladesh as a whole. The new agricultural technologies enabled the 4.5 acre rich farmer to increase his revenues by approximately Rs.

4400 per year. His labor time needs also expanded from 66 to 258 man-days per year. With no substantial increase of fixed costs this farmer's income growth can reasonably be assumed to have been potentially large. At the same time the 1.5 acre small peasant farmer had under traditional technology an expected net revenue of Rs. 740, hardly sufficient to guard against drastic output variations. The irrigation and high-yielding varieties technology tripled the net revenue of this small farmer to Rs. 2460 with an income increase of about Rs. 1720. Modern technology, however, increased the shadow price on land for this 1.5 acre farmer from Rs. 174 to Rs. 628 per acre. The corresponding increase for the 4.5 acre farmer was from Rs. 174 to Rs. 445. Again, if these farmers could borrow on the same basis, the shadow price on land for the poor farmer would far exceed that of the rich farmer: "Thus, *if* divisible modern technology is available to *all*, the pressures for land agglomeration in an unfavorable direction will diminish, since the marginal value of land to the smaller owner-operator is greater than to the capitalist farmer."[1]

Conditions in Bangladesh have deteriorated since 1960. And technology is for the most part *not* available to all, least of all to the subsistence peasant farmer. The document that follows shows not the hypothetical but the real constraints in the transfer of agricultural technology to the poor countries. It is the account of a journalist who visited Bangladesh in early 1975. What he says transcends the fate of the Bangladesh small peasant farmer:

Jamiruddin and his brother inherited two and a half acres each from their father in the rice-growing district of Mymensingh, north of Dacca. Two and a half acres is not enough for a farmer in Bangladesh, where yearly rice yields average 500 kilograms—1,100 pounds per acre, compared with the world average of 1,500 kilograms per acre.

So he and his brother rented more land on the so-called "borga" system, under which the landlord provides the land and gets 50 percent of the harvest while the tenant supplies seed, tools, and fertilizer and does all the work.

His brother continues to make a go of it. But Jamiruddin had a succession of mishaps. First one of his two cows dies. The river shifted, eating away some of the land he had inherited. Of course, this meant new land was created somewhere else. But such land belongs by law to the government and goes in practice to the wealthier members of the community who can afford to bid for it.

Each year Jamiruddin went a bit more into debt—the usual system being that for every 100 takas worth he borrowed before the harvest, he would have to return 150 takas at harvest time four months later. (7.8 takas equals $1 at the inflated official rate.) Gradually, reluctantly, he sold off his land, sliver by sliver, as if slicing off his very flesh and bone, and knowing that once gone he could never afford to buy a parcel back.

Finally, he was entirely a tenant farmer; he had no land left of his own. Then came the great flood of 1974, destroying Jamiruddin's hut and washing away his tools. He gathered up wife and five children, sold the pitiful bits and pieces of tools and utensils he had left and fled southward to Dacca aboard a free government train. If and when he can find work as a day laborer, he will earn from five to six takas (nominally worth about 75 cents, actually worth probably one-third of this amount) a day. How long would it take him to earn the money to become a tenant farmer again? "Allah knows," says Jamiruddin, inclining his head.[2]

Mexico

The Mexican peasant paid dearly for the land he owns or cultivates today. By 1910 there were some 15 million landless peasants in Mexico while 11,000 landlords possessed about 57 percent of the land.[3] This intolerable situation was changed by the peasant revolution of 1910 that lasted for almost a decade. Mexican land reform has been going on ever since. And yet today in Mexico it is the large landholder who monopolizes water and other agricultural resources.[4] Mexico has many rural landless laborers. It also has as many peasants practicing subsistence agriculture today as in 1910.[5] Neither the private smallholders nor those peasants cultivating communal land *(ejidatarios)* benefit much from rural education and extension services. And since the small Mexican farmer can only turn to the government for credit, that financial resource has been limited, sporadic, and, until recently, restricted only to crop loans. If these difficulties were not enough, the small peasant farmer has little access to irrigated water. In Mexico as well as in some other countries of Latin America water cannot be privately owned. The governments in that region will not make water available to farmers unless those governments' cropping patterns are accepted.[6] It is no wonder, then, that the lands benefiting from the extensive irrigation works in Mexico are owned for the most part by that country's political elite or their relatives and friends.[7]

The green revolution was born in Mexico. Yet, given the position of the small farmer in the Mexican social structure, it is not surprising to learn that he benefited the least from the green revolution technology. Concentrated as he is in the traditional agricultural regions, with a small plot to cultivate and with limited credit sources at his disposal, the small Mexican peasant farmer did not even manage to grow wheat, the most profitable of the green revolution foodcrops. This is because wheat became the high-yielding crop of the large farmer living in the Pacific North and North regions. The distribution of agricultural inputs, land tenure patterns, and production practices favored northern Mexico and its new commercial agricultural elite. Alone in Latin America, this elite has won unprecedented privileges. It pays low taxes and low wages, earns high profits, and commands the services of a public infrastructure.[8]

The spread of agricultural technology has been sporadic and uneven among various Latin American countries. Argentina, for instance, with all its biological potential has had low agricultural productivity. The problem here is one of structural political weakness that has not adjusted to modern needs.[9] It appears, then, that the underdeveloped countries' governmental attitudes are very critical to the transfer of agricultural technology. "The classic case is Argentina—a nonparticipator in the new technology, despite enormous land and water resources and the proved suitability of the new technology. All because of negative and restrictive government policy."[10]

During the two decades before 1968, the Latin American region increased its supplies of chemical fertilizers nearly eight times, while the number of farm tractors more than quadrupled. Mexico tripled its wheat yields, while Brazil's wheat output remained unchanged. Chile tripled its corn yields, Argentina doubled its corn production, but Brazil did not exceed a modest 10 percent growth in the same foodgrain. The same contrast is evident in cattle production. The few efficient, high quality livestock farms lose their significance in comparison with the average cattle farm of very low productivity levels. And yet it is on those few farms that command modern management, capital, and technology that the increases in crop and livestock production have taken place. This development has resulted in increased unemployment in the context of decreasing market opportunities for traditional agriculture, and of a growing rural labor force.[11] The fact that slightly over 100 farms, of about 200 hectares in size each, could produce nearly one-third of all the rice grown in Venezuela[12] indicates that technological change in that country was unbalanced. The few produced the most and received the most from the wealth of applied technology. The job of the 100 farms could have been accomplished by a greater number of farms with the beneficial return that many more farmers would have been involved in the generation and distribution of agricultural income. As it is, the 100 Venezuelan farmers are typical of the social structure and of the beneficiaries of agricultural technology in Latin America:

> Over two-thirds of the Latin American agricultural population—about 70 million people—receive an annual income averaging less than 100 dollars per person. The per capita income of approximately half of this

group is probably less than 50 to 60 dollars per year. This income barely permits subsistence. At the same time, a large percentage of the total agricultural income is appropriated by a small minority with the result that their per capita income levels are 50 to 100 times those of the poorest segment of the peasantry.[13]

This small agricultural elite is small indeed. In numbers it includes no more than 2 percent of the farm families of Latin America but in wealth this very small elite owns about 50 percent of all agricultural land. Meanwhile, from one-third to more than half of the rural labor force is for all purposes unemployed.[14] There is, then, an intimate interrelationship between the effects technology has on a particular society and the social structure of that society. "In Latin America modern technology has tended to increase rural unemployment and intensify income concentration."[15]

West Pakistan

Agriculture is the most important single sector of West Pakistan economy. It is responsible for 75 percent of the foreign exchange earnings and provides the livelihood for about 70 percent of the population. Much of the industrial activity in West Pakistan is also focused on agricultural goods and services.[16]

West Pakistan is fortunate to have rich water resources. Within its 200 million acres lie the Indus Plains with the world's largest irrigation system, commanding as it does some 33.5 million acres. It is the Indus River and its major tributaries that provide an immense supply of water to the Indus Plains. Nearly 70 percent of West Pakistan's cultivated land is to be found within the Indus Plains. This cultivated area yields about 80 percent of all food produced in West Pakistan. Needless to say, a large majority of the population lives where most of the foodcrops are grown.[17]

The part of the Indus Basin that today barely feeds West Pakistan was once the granary of India. It produced enough wheat to meet the needs of the subcontinent and to fuel a prosperous export trade. It has been suggested that West Pakistan's wheat deficiencies in the years 1950–1965 might be an indirect result of the easy terms of U.S. wheat supplies.[18] Yet the fact remains that the farmer in West Pakistan attains very low yields in both irrigated and nonirrigated land. His farming and irrigation practices are inefficient. He fails to adequately use fertilizers, plant protection, and other inputs. He also gives little attention to land leveling, seed-bed preparation, and weed control; and he does not take care of his land after cultivation.[19] The 1960 Pakistan Census of Agriculture shows that about half of the farms are under five acres in size. This, however, accounts for only 10 percent of the cultivable area, leaving much of the farm area in relatively large farms. Absentee landowners own large farms ranging from more than 500 acres of irrigated to 1,000 acres of nonirrigated land.[20] In this land tenure system, sharecropping "is widely practiced, with its attendant ills of insecurity of tenure, inadequate investment in production facilities, and limited rewards to the actual cultivators."[21]

POVERTY AND CAPITAL-INTENSIVE TECHNOLOGIES

India's is "a poverty-stricken, elite-ridden rural economy."

> Her five-year plans have sought to bring together Soviet-style planning with heavy emphasis on the public sector and heavy industries, Ghandian-style approach to village industries centering on the spinning wheel, Western-style theorizing along with macro-economic model-building, and colonial style financing with a tight treasury grip on public expenditures.[22]

In this context India launched a new agricultural strategy during 1965–1966. The purpose of this strategy was to facilitate agricultural modernization, especially where assured rainfall or irrigation facilities existed. The emphasis of this strategy was on the availability of a package of practices and production inputs. It was assumed that profitability at the micro or farm level would follow. India was hit by drought during the period of 1965–1967. The following year the high-yielding varieties technology enabled India to produce a total of 96 million metric tons of foodgrain. By 1971–1972 the area under green revolution was increased considerably. Equally impressive was the nearly 40 percent increase in the area of multiple cropping that was brought under cultivation in just seven years after the new agricultural strategy was put into effect. With about 75 percent of the land under cultivation lacking irrigation, the element of weather will continue to be an unpredictable and disturbing factor in India's total foodgrain production.[23]

India's is a political economy whose two crucial unresolved problems are rapid population growth and an inelastic supply of land. The introduction of the green revolution biological technology helped India to increase its foodgrain output. In fact, the 1965 new agricultural strategy was simply a method designed to institutionalize the benefits of the high-yielding foodcrops technology. The Indian government decided that mechanization was necessary in order to maintain the impetus of the new green revolution technology. By 1971 tractors in India increased by more than 100 percent from the 1956 level. The states of Punjab and Haryana accounted for more than 42 percent of the total tractors in India. Indeed, Punjab doubled its tractor population both during the periods of 1956 to 1961 and 1961 to 1966.[24]

The rapid agricultural mechanization of Punjab inevitably raised the question of the desirability of a capital-intensive technology in a country with abundant labor and increasing rural unemployment. No sufficient data exist to answer this question. But if one considers the same question in the context of the prosperous Punjab then it appears that its tractors did benefit multiple and intensive cropping. They contributed to increased production and gave jobs to hired workers. Yet the "intimate interrelationship" that exists between farm intensification and mechanization might easily be upset[25] with the result that unemployment will become in Punjab as bad a nightmare as in the rest of India. The intimate interrelationship between poverty and too many machines is above all fragile. In India

[f]arm mechanization so far has supported farm intensification in areas where irrigation has led to a new potential for crop intensification and the projected demand for labor is much more than the number of agricultural labor available. However, the degree of mechanization should not go beyond a point where the bargaining power of agricultural labor is in any way undermined. Appropriate public policies can assist in this by seeing that (1) tractorization is selective in those areas where conditions for tractorization are favorable and (2) misallocation of investment or tractors in those areas where conditions are not too favorable is minimized.[26]

DISTRIBUTING THE BENEFITS OF TECHNICAL INNOVATIONS

It is a simple fact that the poor countries will never manage to grow enough food until they can efficiently manage their scarce scientific talent and institutional resources for agricultural research. Research must be organized and operated so that it generates more research capacity. Allocating research resources for agricultural modernization is not merely a technical and scientific proposition imperfectly understood; it is also a social issue and policy with profound implications for the distribution of income:

To consider aggregated representative farms in a context divorced from the social milieu within which they operate may lead to technologic choices having disastrous social consequences. Without extraordinary

care, government investments in capital-intensive schemes with a high
foreign exchange component, in credit programs controlled by "local
influential people," in water control projects which neglect to consider
the position of the landless and near-landless, or in infrastructure (like
rural electrification and many road schemes) that primarily benefits the
relatively well-to-do while taxing the poor peasants, will lead to further
consolidation of power of the exploiting classes. Within rural society in
Bangladesh, there are already serious class differences. A magnification
of these class differences is inevitable unless the impoverished realize
their potential political power. Otherwise, technologic choices will be
made by a political system reflecting narrow class interests and will
nullify fragile gains which benefit all.[27]

There is no doubt that an existing unequal distribution in assets and
income may be reinforced by a new technology that increases the
returns of a particular factor of production. This real possibility of
technological change properly channeled can then offer the opportunity to direct the distribution of income to a desired social goal. The
very choice of regions, crops, and scientific disciplines for the execution
of agricultural research will have an impact on the income and relations between tenant and landlord and the rest of the members of the
community.

And that is precisely what happened with the spread of the green
revolution technologies. Given the glaring inequalities in the social
structures of the poor countries using these new high-yielding foodgrain technologies, the rich benefited most. To those who have been
vocal about this injustice, a member of the American scientific community, intimately involved with the genesis and development of the
green revolution, said: "[I]f less unequal income distribution is desired
why not simply redistribute the land?" He further added:

> New technology changes the distribution of income because it increases
> the relative productivity and demand for various factors of production. If
> all factors were equally owned or if all income were equally divided then
> there would be no skewing of income one way or another by change in
> technology. Thus it is the imposition of change in factor shares on an
> existing inequality which creates the problem. Clearly to diffuse re-
> search attention from increasing output per unit of input to additional
> concern with the bias in factor shares reduces the accomplishment on the
> primary objectives.[28]

A poor country, then, should welcome technical innovation only
when the benefits of the new technological change are distributed to
those who formerly were responsible for the arduous task taken over
by the new technology. In a communal society the freeing of mothers
from manual labor provides opportunities for child care. In a society of

inequality the replacement of labor-intensive tasks with machinery simply eliminates the source of income for those who need it most. It also increases the net income of the higher income consuming and producing members of the society.[29]

INCREASING DEMAND FOR FOOD AND
EXTREMELY LOW YIELDS

The world food problem and a rapid population growth have greatly intensified demand for food. Poor countries either do not have enough to eat or find it impossible to meet their food needs by a greater use of production factors in the context of fixed land base and without new higher yielding technologies. The poor people in the poor countries spend a great deal of their income on food. In India, while the rich spent only two percent of their income growth on foodgrain, the poor had to allocate 59 percent of the increase to their financial resources for the same purpose.[30] The rising but just expectations of the poor for more food adds another dimension to the need for technical change in the underdeveloped nations as a precondition for a higher yielding agricultural technology.

In Asia rice production is falling behind the growing demand for this critical foodcrop. The Asian farmer apparently is not accepting and utilizing the technological innovations in rice production at a rate that could balance production and demand. The high-yielding foodcrops in India since 1972 have become increasingly less productive. They have been attacked by various diseases and other yield-limiting factors. Data for the whole of India also indicate that since 1973 fertilizer use has been leveling off. But above all it is the inflexible institutional structure that hinders the Indian peasant from adopting the new technologies.[31] Even in the Philippines, the home of the International Rice Research Institute, there is a disturbing "gap" between the farmer's yield and the biological potential. Some of the constraints that help to explain why the farmer in the Philippines is getting very low returns include: (1) use of varieties lacking resistance to pests, diseases, and lodging (technological constraints); (2) the use of mixed varieties and old seedlings, poor weed and insect control, improper timing of fertilizer application (management constraints); (3) soil problems (for instance, zinc deficiency) and inadequately controlled water supplies (environmental constraints).[32] Yet the Philippines is not a typical underdeveloped country thanks to her long association with the United States:

> Philippines has been active and fairly successful in agricultural development. She is a pot bubbling to some extent but, perhaps, not evenly.

Some of the constraints to agricultural technology transfer have been tackled in the Philippines. The country is a laboratory. And she has plenty of educated agricultural scientists.[33]

In most of the poor countries the yields in agriculture are extremely low. The availability of a large labor force has in no way made the agriculture of the underdeveloped nations labor-intensive. This is perhaps because too many rural people do not work at all, and those who do cultivate the land do so inefficiently. And the power elite of these non-Western countries do very little to advance the lot of the rural poor. In fact, their development policies are designed to benefit what they conceive to be their own interests and not those of the majority they govern. The key to agricultural modernization is no less than sustained reforms of the entire institutional structure so that the peasant farmer can live and work in an environment congenial to opportunity for betterment:

> In agriculture there is need for a changed relation between man and land, creating the possibilities and the incentives for man to work harder and more effectively and investing whatever he can to improve the land. Without fundamental reforms of land ownership, strivings for "community development" have proved ineffectual. The whole educational system should be changed. This amounts to much more than placing additional children into schools. In most underdeveloped countries the school systems have changed little from colonial and quasicolonial times. Schools support the inherited grossly inegalitarian social and economic stratification and among other things, the prejudice against manual work. Education as a whole is now often anti-developmental in its effect.[34]

DEVELOPMENT OF AGRICULTURAL RESOURCES

The equal distribution and development of the agricultural resources of the poor countries appear to be logical steps for ending hunger and poverty for the majority of mankind. A labor-intensive agricultural economy based on an institutional and social arrangement favoring the peasant farmer is a necessary precondition for agricultural modernization. The poor countries consume 181 kilograms of all grains per capita per year. While Japan, Korea, and Taiwan have had the export earnings to import food and foodgrains, the countries of Southeast Asia have either declining or vanishing exportable surpluses of rice. And South Asia has also moved dramatically from a net surplus position to one of hunger and famine. "Increasing the output of food crops in Asia means primarily increasing the output on small farms, using labor-intensive and energy-saving methods."[35] The rich countries can best help the underdeveloped world with their scientific and technological knowledge in making it possible that the agriculture of the poor nations has adequate genetic variability and supplies of energy and fertilizer. That precisely should be one of the goals of the transfer of agricultural science and technology to the non-Western world.

Chapter 6

What Is to Be Done: Traditional Agricultural Systems and New Technology

PROTEIN SOURCES OF THE POOR COUNTRIES

Cereals provide the mainstay of the diet for the majority of the people in the poor countries. These foodgrains supply about 52 percent of the calories and nearly half of the total protein of the nutritional needs of the poor in the underdeveloped nations. Foodgrain production "has barely kept pace with population and income growth during recent years" in these food-deficit regions of the world. Failure to meet domestic demands for cereals led a number of low-income countries to increase imports of these critical foodgrains with the result that much-needed capital for social and economic development had to be spent for food imports. It is also true that "cereals are the lynchpin of the cropping system in many developing countries and contribute significantly to income and employment." In the past, many of these countries managed to increase their food production simply by expanding their cultivated areas. This is still the case for some countries that have the good fortune to possess additional land reserves. But for most of the poor countries no more good land exists to be brought into production. They are now pressing against the limits of their natural resources. It is obvious, then, that existing and new technologies are necessary to increase the yields and limit the time of maturity of these foodgrains. Occupying as they do the largest area of land under cultivation in a variety of environments, cereals "hold the key to the more effective use of land and water resources." Failure to modernize the foodgrain production of the poor countries will make it even more difficult to advance the cultivation of other crops or make livestock production more efficient since most of the land will be used to satisfy basic calorie needs.[1]

For most of the poor in the underdeveloped countries, food legumes are the second main source of protein. They add the much needed amino acids that their cereals diet fails to supply. Food legumes also have the potential to become the source for simulated milk and meat products. This could especially benefit pregnant women and infants and introduce millions to animal protein that today, even if it is available, is not consumed for various religious, physiological, and other reasons. Increasing productivity of most grain legumes in the tropics will continue to challenge the best creative minds in agricultural science and technology. It appears that these legumes have "intractable physiological and morphological problems which might impose a low ceiling on yields even if pest and disease control measures were highly efficient." These problems make grain legumes poor beneficiaries of irrigation, fertilizer, and other inputs. Moreover, many species of food legumes have no *ecological* common denominator.[2]

Starchy foods including roots and tubers are of great dietary value to millions of people in the poor countries, especially in tropical equatorial Africa. Potentially they can be made to produce "an enormous output of energy per hectare." Technologies are also developing to raise the yield and nutritional quality and to expand the range of adaptation of this major group of foodcrops. Yet these crops, with the exception of potato, were never part of the diet of the rich countries, with the result that "they have received much less concentrated research attention than the cereals."[3]

In some of the poorest of the poor countries, like those in the Sahelian region of Africa, ruminants of all other livestock "are of dominant social and economic significance." To a limited extent ruminants compete with man for food. But given the fact that some of the poorest and most backward countries have few if any opportunities for agricultural development, ruminants have the potential to utilize existing resources effectively and give those countries a needed source of animal protein. For these reasons the global network of agricultural research has only recently invested resources to study "predominant *systems* of livestock production in Africa." The idea here is to develop and introduce new technologies for each system of livestock production:

> This approach is to an important extent a reversal of the procedure adopted by some of the older International Centers which started by focussing on achieving a technical breakthrough on a rather narrow

front, and have only recently placed greater emphasis on trying to influence traditional systems to accommodate this new technology.[4]

MAXIMIZING THE USE OF SCARCE RESOURCES

The technological philosophy of the international agricultural research institutes was, and to a great extent still is, commodity- and problem-oriented. "Successes of the international centres have thus far been achieved mainly by programmes sharply focused on an individual crop."[5] Certainly such a procedure has the advantage of simplicity, clarity, and easy definition. With each new high-yielding variety of wheat, maize, or rice developed, the research institutes presented the farmer with an integrated "package" of technology appropriate to the new foodcrop. Yet such a simple approach is often inadequate:

> Except in monocultures, water use and management has to be related to the crop-mix rather than to the individual crop; fertilizer and pesticide residues contributing to environmental pollution again come from the totality of the farm and not just one enterprise. The introduction of small-scale livestock often implies a major revision of an established system. Multiple cropping depending on high output her annum involves radically different management *and* plant breeding and cultural concepts than systems which depend principally on high yield per individual crop. Inadequate survey and exploration of surface and sub-surface water resources combined with insufficient research on soil/plant/water relationships is frequently a serious obstacle to sound design, good water management and the development of optimum production systems in irrigated areas. Storage, and control of certain causes of crop loss, e.g. rodents, may present problems of a broader nature than a single crop. The recent critical world grain reserve situation has called attention to the need for improvement of storage, and the prevention of post-harvest losses, and while some of the problems may require mainly the application of existing knowledge for their solution, there are undoubtedly crops and situations for which more research is needed—for example, storage of roots and tubers on small farms. However, storage and its related problems may often form only one component of a much larger post-harvest system, and consideration therefore needs to be given to approaching this system in its totality having regard to uses of commodities for food, feed, and technical purposes, along multi-disciplinary lines, in much the same way as we are now attacking the problems of production prior to harvest.[6]

Certainly the commodity-oriented package approach to agricultural change and modernization is not likely to succeed in areas like the

Near East and North Africa where needs dictate that raising the yields of a single crop is secondary to the urgent task of *intensifying* agriculture and increasing *productivity* through better resource utilization. "The concept of high yields per individual crop which has so far dominated the goals of the older institutes may have to be subordinated to one of maximizing the use of scarce resources—in this region, generally water." This means that technologies have to be developed to integrate crops and livestock, to accommodate changes in cropping patterns in irrigated land in order to optimize income and employment, and, in general, to benefit productive systems of individual foodcrops, livestock, and nonfood for forage crops.

> But although increasing yields and production of basic staple foods must remain a priority goal, the ultimate objective of agricultural research is development and the economic well-being of people. We must not be so bewitched with the hopes of further spectacular successes with single crops that we fail to recognize that other pathways to growth may exist. In some regions, for ecological, social, or economic reasons, research of a broader nature—even if it appears more complex, may offer the better hope of a solution.[7]

It is the international centers in the Philippines (IRRI) and in Mexico (CIMMYT) that have shaped the technological and institutional philosophy of the global network of agricultural research. They and their commodity-package-oriented research became the paradigm for the newer centers. It is true that these younger institutes deviated to some degree from the IRRI-CIMMYT limited commodity model with their responsibilities for multiple products. They still have not had the time to prove themselves or to generate their own working philosophies. This is reflected in the fact that the "early successes" of these tropical research centers were "in commodity programmes such as rice and maize, for which the institutes serve as relay stations and area adaptation centres for the work of CIMMYT and IRRI."[8] So powerful an appeal does the high-yielding technologies paradigm have on those who founded the older two institutes that in a sense they question the proposition that the new "tropical research stations" can become effective in their total farming systems commitments:

> It remains to be demonstrated . . . whether a centre can retain the power of its concentration and specialisation while simultaneously moving into the much wider area of total farming systems. It is our judgement that this approach will function more effectively if the centre focuses on analyses to delimit and resolve major impediments to the production of a few important products. Of necessity, research on the

broader range of commodities within the system will be carried out in large measure by national research organizations. A systems approach to research by an international centre tends to force the development of an interrelated set of national and more locally-specific research stations, as has already been demonstrated by the CIMMYT and IRRI experience.[9]

It may be that this thesis has some validity. It is not likely, however, that the new tropical institutes will remain the satellites of IRRI and CIMMYT for long. To do so would defeat the purpose of their creation. It is also not likely that the national research organizations perceive themselves as members of a "system" guided by IRRI or CIMMYT. Besides, national research capabilities are hardly in a position to conduct "research on the broader range of commodities within the system." At the same time it cannot be assumed that institutes like IRRI and CIMMYT will be generating similar centers for research. In fact, their philosophies, if not their existence, have been questioned by the leadership of the global network within which they still are the classic paradigms of international institutional agricultural research:

It is undeniable that large multidisciplinary institutes are costly to establish, expensive to run, and hard to disengage from or to alter the course of if they cease to be highly productive. There are also problems of site-specificity in the results, where research is centralised largely at one location. This has led to doubts about continuing to add to their number, and to a search for other institutional approaches to international or regional research which are cheaper or more flexible.[10]

And yet the predicament of the international research centers is not of their own making alone. It is also the predicament of the rich countries that have not allocated the resources necessary "to interrelate the agricultural technologies available into acceptable sociological and economic packages."

We have often been forced to offer subsistence farmers technological packages that they cannot afford and, therefore, will not use. We are forced to do this because in view of impending world food shortages, we have had to constantly stress maximum yields to farmers who are more concerned with minimum risks. We have demonstrated that monoculture agriculture can be highly efficient even in the tropics with the proper technology, but we have been able to do very little to develop improved technological packages for use with multiple or mixed cropping systems which are predominant in the tropics. As agricultural scientists, we know that diversity is the safest way of preventing total crop failures but we also realize the difficulty involved in studying individual crops.

The difficulties increase as we begin to integrate 2, 3 or more crops; so with the limited manpower available we have been forced to work on one crop at a time. Unless the proportion of our national and international budgets spent on agriculture research is increased we won't even be able to maintain the agricultural scientists necessary to do the job, much less can we contemplate expansion to integrate vitally needed social scientists into the world food production problem. If you compare the scope of the budgets for Departments of Defense, NASA (in its prime) or even for medical research to our agricultural research budgets, you will find out why the job of transferring agricultural technology has not been completely successful. Even in countries that are facing starvation, more money is often spent on defense or even national airlines than on agricultural research.[11]

RATIONAL AGRICULTURAL TECHNOLOGY

Neither the majority of the poor countries nor the international agricultural research centers have the capacity or are willing to undertake fundamental research in the basic sciences that underpin agriculture. For many underdeveloped nations this issue might seem irrelevant, given the fact that their actual yields and cropping intensities are so far below the demonstrated experimental potential. But even those few underdeveloped countries like Egypt, Korea, Taiwan, and parts of India that have used new foodcrop technologies effectively are beginning to press against the limits of their natural resources. They can perhaps further increase the yields of their foodgrains, but only at progressively higher costs and not without the development of entirely new technologies. "It is increasingly being asked whether, in terms of environmental degradation and the use of dwindling world reserves of fossil fuels and other natural resources (phosphates), the high yield technology is the road not to progress but to disaster." The existence of the world food problem makes it even more imperative that new technologies be devised that are capable of helping the farmer to raise enough food without the extensive use of manufactured inputs.[12]

In the underdeveloped nations the possibility exists that the "poor people can be priced right out of the food market and perhaps flood the cities with more and more people."[13] The limited modernizing activities of these countries were undertaken for the sake of modernization itself. They were not intended to increase crop production.[14] Perhaps the poor countries can learn and benefit from the agricultural technology of early twentieth century Europe. With low mechanization European agriculture returned high yields. Farms were labor-intensive. And to reduce fertilizer needs European farmers recycled animal and crop wastes. To effectively utilize this "rational agricultural technol-ogy" would mean that tractors ought to be used for heavy plowing, leaving lighter tasks to draft animals and manpower. Electrical power would also do the job of threshing. The result of such a policy would be high productivity with low energy needs: approximately five kilo-calories (Kcals) of output to each Kcal of input. This rational agri-cultural technology would immediately become "at least twice as productive as current high energy U.S. agriculture."[15] It is important to understand the relationship between ecological energy and eco-nomic accounting:

> ecological accounting of energy inputs and outputs of an agroecosystem provides greater understanding of the interrelationships and mecha-nisms underlying various crop production alternatives. By using this information and assigning current or projected prices for input fuel Kcal and output corn Kcal, sound economic accounting results. Hence, com-bining ecological and economic information significantly strengthens our overall decision making process.[16]

DEVELOPMENT OF A NEW AGRICULTURAL SCIENCE

"The most surprising fact about agriculture is that it sometimes feeds people, that hunger is not more widespread than it is. This is surpris-ing because in most of the world today food production is not engaged in to feed people, food does not flow from well-fed areas to hungry areas; fluctuations in food production do not follow changing needs."[17] This means that food as a commodity has more importance than food as nutrition; and that land is considered more as an investment than as productive soil. In this context science is used to advance the goals of political economy and not those necessary to achieve freedom from hunger.[18]

In the tropics, however, agriculture does largely serve immediate human needs. And since the scientific understanding of tropical ag-riculture is still minimal, it is not only possible but necessary that a new agricultural science develop with the purpose of meeting the food requirements of the majority of mankind. Here it is important to stress that such a development ought not to separate biology from its social and political matrix. Only then can we hope to understand agriculture, and in the process transform it in a positive and critical way that can benefit the small peasant farmer. *To maintain agricultural research within the existing social and land tenure structures of the poor coun-tries is to reinforce those prevailing arrangements and limit the imagi-*

nation and scope of agricultural science and technology to the narrowly practical. The alternative to this confining procedure is to support research which will look at the complex system of economic reality and ecological necessity. The conflicts that are likely to be resolved by such a challenging social and scientific approach will inevitably become the instruments of change.[19] It is here that Western resources, both human and material, can have an impact on the solution of the world food problem and on the critical and humane evolution of the whole of mankind. It is a fact that the West has been the school of the non-Western peoples. It is also a fact that even the American agricultural research community is dominated by a dogmatic ideology that emphasizes pragmatism at the expense of theory. This means that advances in genetics and ecology are used by agricultural workers, but without their necessary reworking to make them useful:

> Therefore dramatic advances in plant breeding such as the development of the new high-yield varieties of wheat, rice, and corn have been the result of massive varietal testing and crossing with only negligible use of any insights after Mendel's.[20] Meanwhile in the urban centers of "fundamental" research there is little incentive or interest in serving agriculture, and a strong snobbery toward applied research, toward organisms of economic significance, and toward colleagues in these areas.[21]

That such should be the behavior and direction within the West's leading agricultural research establishment is bad enough. But while the rich nations have the potential to correct this misdirection of scientific effort, the poor countries, tempted as they are by the affluence of their tutors, are not in a position to transcend the paradigm of Western agricultural research once they transplant it to their national research systems. The world food problem adds such an urgency to the pressing food needs of these developing areas that it is tempting to believe that basic research done elsewhere can be applied to a nontemperate region:

> But the basic research needed for tropical agriculture is yet to be carried out. The pattern of U.S. agriculture—the introduction of large scale commercial farming based on very high input of energy, chemicals, and machinery—is a dangerous one: it creates dependence on imports, threatens the ecology and health, exhausts the soil, and perpetuates the intellectual colonialism which is retarding the development of new centers of scientific imagination.[22]

The point here is not that the poor countries have nothing to learn from the technologically advanced nations or that the U.S. agricultural research did not help food production. Rather, the idea advanced is that Western agricultural research in its American model is self-limiting. Structurally and ideologically it is committed to "short-term one-step modification of existing agricultural systems." This method pays little attention to the indirect consequences of individual changes while it largely ignores the possibilities of theoretical work in genetics and ecology. Moreover, the pragmatic and empirical components of the existing tradition in U.S. agricultural research tend to fragmentize agricultural science and in the process to lose sight of an important element in global perspective.[23] If the purpose of agriculture is that of feeding people, then its research strategy must emphasize whole system analysis that crosses disciplines and rejects the dichotomy of fundamental versus applied research. This is especially crucial for the poor countries. They have too few trained agricultural scientists. No crash program could possibly meet the needs they have in modernizing their agriculture. Instead, what these countries must do is to restructure their research so that they can effectively mobilize their total intellectual resources.[24] China seems to provide a paradigm in that direction.

✳ *Chapter 7*

What Is to Be Done: Commitments to Benefit the Rural Poor

GLOBAL POVERTY AND HUMAN SURVIVAL

The precarious imbalance between the small group of elites that benefit in wealth, income, and power from new technology and the rural majorities of the underdeveloped countries cannot last for long. Gunnar Myrdal, the Nobel Prize Swedish economist, sees in the poverty imbalance of the poor countries a danger far transcending the borders of those nations. Once again in early 1975 Myrdal repeated his thesis on world poverty: "Without conquering mass poverty in the world, there are indeed present trends that even can call in question the survival of the human race or large parts of it."[1] Similarly motivated, Robert McNamara, president of the World Bank, said in effect that the time has come for the governments of the underdeveloped countries to be

> willing to make strong commitments to pursue agricultural strategies directed toward the promotion of new income and employment opportunities for the poorest groups. They must commit themselves to effective land reform, assurance of adequate credit at reasonable cost, and reassessment of pricing taxation, and subsidy policies that discriminate against the rural areas.[2]

LAND REFORM WITH TEETH

What for McNamara is an "effective land reform," for a student of Indian development and an Indian economist himself becomes a "land reform with teeth":

133

This means abolition of absentee landlordism in whatever form, imposition of meaningful ceilings rigidly enforced, and family holdings for "owner-cultivation" strictly defined. Such reforms will provide the best guarantee against blind mechanization and consequent displacement of labour, a danger which has already become real in some areas . . . . Land-reform-with-teeth . . . . will end the domination of the poor by the rural elite, which has perpetrated so much injustice and misery in rural India . . . . It will end the fiscal bleeding to which the economy has been subjected by the affluent farmers who grow rich on subsidized services, refuse to pay taxes, and use political muscles to thwart all proposals to tax agricultural incomes.[3]

ORGANIZATION AND TECHNOLOGY

It has clearly been shown that the poor peasant farmer of the underdeveloped countries can benefit from new technologies, provided he has access to an organizational structure that will make available to him credit and the needed inputs (seed, fertilizer, water, herbicides, pesticides) and instruct him on the precise use of those inputs. To fail to do so or to assume that the illiterate peasant alone can utilize these complicated and energy-intensive technologies is to court even greater social inequality. Jean Mayer, a Harvard University scientist with knowledge and experience in the social and scientific implications of the world food problem, has put the idea of wealth, poverty, and technology this way:

Large landowners with money to invest can increase their wealth so much faster than small farmers that they are soon in a position to buy them out. This creates a class of landless peasants who starve in the villages or pile up, unemployed, in these gigantic cities which are growing in nightmarish fashion on the coastlines of poor continents. (Premature mechanization, usually introduced by large landowners, also brings about rural unemployment.)[4]

Mayer's is also a correct understanding of what in fact the new agricultural technologies mean and imply:

What one is dealing with is not simply the replacement of one variety of seed by another, but a technological and social revolution. Failure of a single factor in this complex system is enough to compromise the success of agricultural development. And the rate of change required is unprecedented in history.[5]

Mayer is equally emphatic on the question of agricultural technology transfer to the poor countries:

The success of agricultural science and technology transfer largely depends on the interest and willingness of the recipient country to accept such knowledge and provide the organization for its utilization. The problem of technology transfer is basically a problem of the small landowner in the underdeveloped regions. Poor countries cannot undertake the education of each farmer. A grouping of small farmers, a cooperative, is necessary in order to share both the information and the new technology of modern agriculture and food production. For instance, irrigation is a collective responsibility and action. And while centralization facilitates fertilizer availability, decentralization is conducive to the management of agriculture. The water supplies of first-century Rome, their administration and economics, show a technically underdeveloped country's successful effort to provide the vital services of adequate water to a large metropolis. The administrator who ran that public sector service was Sextus Julius Frontinus (ca. 40–105). His was a sophisticated and economically efficient administration of the water supplies of Rome. Frontinus' *De aquis urbis Romae* (*On the Water Supplies of Rome*) is an important account of an important public health administration service. Poor country civil servants and administrators can profitably read Frontinus' work. Men like Frontinus are in short supply in the underdeveloped world. Poor countries have gaps in technology, availability of management and social organization. Agricultural modernization in both Taiwan and China shows that official ideology is not a limiting factor when the needs of the farmers have been given the priority they deserve. When Mao Tse-tung sent the Chinese intelligentsia to the villages he accomplished two basic things: (1) he brought the elite in immediate contact with the problems of the majority and (2) he helped the development of leadership at the local level. In contrast to China, the underdeveloped world has no agricultural leadership. China and the rest of the socialist countries have shown that they are more receptive than the non-socialist poor countries to attack malnutrition. The United States must assume the leadership to solve the world food problem. Pressure must be put on both the rich and the poor countries to cooperate in an effort to make the underdeveloped nations food efficient.[6]

HALF-FAMISHED AND HALF-FED

Committed as he is to help the malnourished and the poor, Mayer was disappointed with the 1974 Rome Food Conference.[7] He said that at the Rome Food Conference

[t]he United States pledged less food aid than in any year since World War II. Europe (East and West) pledged almost nothing. The Russians pledged nothing and refused, once again, to even divulge the size of their reserves, which they deem a "military secret." The Chinese proclaimed that any talk of population control was "genocidal" and recipient coun-

tries, instead of pledging maximum efforts to achieve self-sufficiency, excused their shortcomings by blasting the wasteful practices of the rich countries, a legitimate object of irritation but not a justification for inadequate efforts.[8]

It is not difficult to understand Mayer's disappointment. At the Rome Food Conference the delegates from 130 nations had to confront the unpleasant fact that the world as it is, is half-famished and half-fed. That the conference even convened was an important accomplishment in itself. This is how another American participant reacted to what he saw at the Rome Food Conference:

> Looking back on all this, I think the food conference did a good job in centering attention on the immediate emergency. But the longer problem remains—how to feed a swelling population on a small planet with finite resources. America cannot continue much longer as world food bank, as it has for 25 years; the problem is too big. Social revolutions are required right back in the poor countries themselves to free the small farmer and the landless, loinclothed laborer.[9]

WORLD FOOD SECURITY SYSTEM

It may be that "America cannot continue much longer as world food bank," and yet she must. The Rome Food Conference resolutions may or may not result in a functioning world food security system. The United States does have the scientific, management, and food potential to create a food security system with the cooperation of the food-rich countries. The power of this system can be used not merely in emergencies but *to put enough pressure on the food-deficit nations to modernize their agriculture while they reform their social structures.* Time for diplomatic niceties and "strategic" considerations is slowly running out as more and more millions of people are born to face starvation.

Without design the United States became the dominant world food power. American soybeans are part of the diet of a billion Asians. Japanese livestock depends on American feed grains. And the management of the U.S. surplus stock of grain does affect the price of food the world over. This means that the U.S. is both the world food supplier and the world food price stabilizer. It need not be said that from that position of power the U.S. manages a large part of this planet's economy. As long as the grain stock was high in the U.S., the poor of the world had a good chance that food would be made available to them either as a donation or on long term easy payments. Since 1972, however, bad harvests, the price of oil, and huge purchases of U.S. grain by rich countries have essentially punished the poor food-deficit nations. They simply cannot afford to buy grain from the U.S. market. It is here that the issue of a global food security system becomes so crucial. The management and control of food reserves on a worldwide scale must become a top priority of U.S. food policy. Yet the secretary of the U.S. Department of Agriculture, when he considers the question of food reserves at all, feels that those reserves ought to be in private hands.

> He does not accept the prevailing belief that world food stocks are dangerously low. He is afraid of low farm prices, but not, apparently, of high, even exceedingly high, and widely fluctuating, food prices. He seems to make few if any concessions to foreign concern or even the world energy crisis except as it affects U.S. farm interests. There seems to be general agreement that it is impossible in the modern interdependent world for the world grain trade to function under a bare-cupboard policy—no reserve system. Under such circumstances prices would fluctuate widely and wildly. No country could plan for development programs. Grain price fluctuations would affect other commodities. Spreading economic instability would raise the spectre of world political upheaval. Many believe that a world food reserve of some kind is an essential component for satisfactory functioning of the world food market.[10]

Since the mid-1960s the policy of the rich countries to donate food or offer it on concessional sales to the poor countries has increasingly come under question. It was felt that such a policy would in time become too costly to be viable.

The other point undermining food aid is the accepted proposition that food from the industrial nations simply stifled the incentive of the poor countries to increase their food production. Besides, long term concessional sales of food made it possible for various governments to abandon or postpone needed agricultural reforms.[11] Be that as it may, it has been suggested that today "[a]n opportunity exists to call on one great, generally unrecognized, world food reserve—the gap between present low yields in developing countries and what they could be."[12] Whatever the size of the food reserve, it must not be used for political purposes. And if the United States does take the leadership in a global food security system the U.S. government must immediately abandon the tradition of using food to reward "strategic" allies and buy friends. In early March 1975 a commentator made the point that in 1974 "only 37 percent of the main U.S. food program was budgeted for countries officially listed as especially hungry and poor. Congress became so outraged at the political use of food that it passed a law requiring 70 percent of the aid to go to the most needy countries."[13]

Underdeveloped countries are likely to listen to the voice of decency and help their poverty-stricken majorities if they become convinced that those who control the food security system have the welfare of the poor as their main priority. Important as this ethical consideration may be, a world food security system will not function unless a continuous flow of information and reliable analyses on crop conditions, prospects, stock levels, and policies becomes globally institutionalized. Such a massive exchange of data has the potential to bring mankind closer together. It is not easy to think or act on a global scale. Yet the time has come to support the emergence of a global civilization. The world food problem is a major manifestation that science and technology have so shrunk the vast dimensions of this globe that national and regional solutions to problems like poverty or malnutrition are simply inadequate.

 *Conclusion*

The Unfinished Revolution: Constraints and Complexity in Resource Transfers

AGRICULTURE AT THE HANDS OF INDIGENOUS AND FUNCTIONAL COLONIALS

Agriculture in the underdeveloped countries is a museum of backwardness and unpleasant facts. It preserves the abject poverty of millions of men, women, and children. And it safeguards with almost religious tenacity low productivity and work inefficiency. Underdeveloped country intellectuals continue their crusades against colonialism but they resist efforts to decolonize their agriculture. As long as the West held by force the non-Western regions of the globe, Western intellectuals had no difficulty in expounding theories intended to relieve the West of moral responsibility for the poverty of its colonies. They said that the natives' tendency toward idleness, inefficiency, and restricted economic activity was an unchangeable component of their social and religious institutions and traditions. When in the 1940s the Westerners left their colonies, they left behind an elite of native Westernizers who understandably were quick to reject the unflattering theories of their former masters. It did not take much time for the native elites to become the new colonial masters of their own lands. They started their "development projects" profoundly convinced of the wisdom of the Western models of economic development. They reasoned that Western economic growth took centuries to mature. This fact led them to believe that if they could simply close that "time lag," they certainly would be able to catch up with the West. With this gospel at hand, the economic planners of the poor

139

countries proceeded to industrialize in the hope that modernization would somehow follow. But they forgot that it was the scientific and technological revolution that made modernization possible. They also forgot that those societies that chose to enter the modern era had to (1) convert their institutions to new functions; (2) incorporate techniques and structures from abroad; and (3) attain new levels of political development, economic growth, and social mobilization. In short, the poor country elite embarked on modernization but they neglected to take into account that modernization involves a series of changes, not merely in technology but in the social and institutional structure, in knowledge, and in values.

The functional activities of technology are performed by elites. Scientists generate knowledge, industrialists utilize such knowledge, and development administrators allocate resources and make decisions on the transfer of technology and the future of development projects. The social and intellectual constraints of these functional elites rarely allow them to support the social dimensions of change. And when technology is transferred to a poor nation, the international elements responsible for the transfer "tend to reinforce sectoral narrowness and rigidity." This they accomplish by sponsoring "macroeconomic growth decisions, market-oriented developmental priorities, rapid depletion of resources and ecological exploitation, and elite-serving educational and health systems."[1] Governments supporting technical assistance are more interested in diplomatic niceties than the welfare of the rural population of the receiving country. And those of the West who bring technologies to the underdeveloped nations follow established procedures not likely to correct the mismanagement of their know-how in a setting they know precious little about.

Technological modernization in the poor countries follows no abstract principles of public interest. The elite leadership of the underdeveloped nations sees industrialization not only as a way out of poverty but as the only strategy of development that has the blessings of their Western mentors. Meanwhile they neglect their agriculture. The costs of this neglect have been high. In the poor countries it is a nonfarm elite that makes all the policy decisions affecting agriculture; the farmers are not encouraged to make choices. Equally inhibiting to agricultural modernization is the low prestige of agriculture among the educated people of the underdeveloped countries. It is as if secondary education immediately sets apart the son of a farmer from the land. His goal is medicine, law, or engineering, but if the only educational avenue open is that of an agricultural college, his training is largely theoretical and totally divorced from the real needs of his country. This disdainful attitude toward the farm and working with one's hands has contributed enormously to guarantee the survival of stagnant agricultural methods and has damaged the growth of native scientific traditions and institutions. It is not surprising then that the colonial policy of transferring Western agricultural technology to tropical and subtropical regions in order to improve the cash crops outlived the colonial empires in their political setting. The native elites felt that the preservation of such an institution was convenient. It provided the needed cash to buy shiny machinery for the benefit of the nonrural sector. Cash crop technologies also allowed the new colonial elites to leave the abysmal social inequalities of the countryside unchanged. Meanwhile their countries began to import food. The green revolution of the 1960s could not have come to the assistance of the underdeveloped country elites at a more propitious time. It increased the yields of corn, wheat, and rice. And for a moment it appeared as if the new high-yielding varieties (HYVs) of foodcrops could have eliminated hunger without the pains of serious and sustained social reform in the countryside.

EPHEMERAL GOLDEN WHEAT ECONOMIES

For Mexico, Pakistan, and India the 1960s were a golden period for their wheat economies. By 1960 about 90 percent of the total wheat area in Mexico was planted with the HYVs. And in just 20 years ending in 1970 Mexico raised its average wheat yields from 0.94 to 2.9 metric tons per hectare. At the same time its gross production increased from 600,000 to 2.2 million tons. Early in the 1960s the Mexican wheats were transferred to India and Pakistan. Ten years later these HYVs covered 33 percent of the wheat cropland of India and about 50 percent of the wheat area of Pakistan. Average yields in India rose by 42 percent and in Pakistan by 37 percent. In terms of production the Mexican HYVs provided 68 percent of the Indian wheat of 1970–1971 and in Pakistan they generated 60 percent of that year's total wheat supplies. By 1971 green revolution rice and wheat were spread to about 7 percent of the total cereals area covering 21.5 million hectares of cropland in the underdeveloped world but not including the centrally planned economies of China, North Vietnam, North Korea, and Cuba. From the total area planted with wheat and rice, 17.2 percent was allocated to HYVs wheat and 10.2 percent was used for HYVs rice cultivation.[2]

The green revolution remains an unfinished revolution. It brought to the underdeveloped countries more than high-yielding foodcrop varieties. Its technologies work best with the assistance of mechanized

Table C-1.   Changes in Production of Wheat and Rice for Selected Asian Countries, 1960–1961 to 1968–1969

Crop and Country	1960/61— 1964/65	1965/66	1966/67	1967/68	1968/69	Percent Increase 1960/61— 1964/65 to 1968/69
		1960–1961 to 1968–1969				
	Thousands of metric tons					
Wheat						
India	10,809	12,290	10,424	11,393	16,568	53
Pakistan	4,065	4,625	3,951	4,393	6,478	59
Total Asia	52,247	56,388	51,904	58,370	64,071	23
Total World	231,758	247,500	285,500	277,190	309,254	33
Rice						
India	53,105	46,500	45,707	59,300	59,000	11
Pakistan	16,539	17,811	16,424	19,024	19,604	12
Philippines	3,883	4,033	4,165	4,560	4,576	18
Total Asia	141,787	138,060	138,355	159,053	160,835	13
Total World	161,000	159,000	161,000	183,000	186,000	16

Source: F. F. Hill and Lowell S. Hardin, "Crop Production Successes and Emerging Problems in Developing Countries," in *Some Issues Emerging From Recent Breakthroughs in Food Production,* edited by Kenneth L. Turk (Ithaca, N.Y.: New York State College of Agriculture, 1971), p. 4, Table 1.

farming fueled as it must be by a lot of fertilizers and plenty of controlled water supplies. Substituting to a considerable degree capital for labor, the monocropping technologies of the green revolution have cheated the small farmer of his efforts to better his standard of living. They made the wealthy landowner more wealthy but at the expense of the poor. Besides, the crops of the green revolution are genetically vulnerable to insects and disease microorganisms. This untested monoculture farming threatens the traditional but biologically sound intercropping practices of the small farmer. Monocropping technologies equally threaten to diminish the variety of food resources available to the nonaffluent societies. These societies have unwritten but precise rules governing their food systems. Certainly the introduction of green revolution crops into food systems not eclectic enough in the range of new ingredients they could tolerate was hardly appropriate, either as a nutrition intervention or as an effort to expand the available dietary choices.

The green revolution was based on the unsound philosophical premises that what worked for the West had to work for non-Western societies. The architects of the green revolution also assumed that the vast poor rural majorities of the underdeveloped countries not only lacked collective memory but had never had any technical skills that could be of any use. They conveniently forgot that agricultural and food technologies were not suddenly born in the twentieth century.

Table C–2.   Estimated Area Planted to High-Yielding Varieties of Wheat and Rice in the Poor Countries, 1972–1973[a]

Wheat	Hectares	Acres
Asia:		
India	10,236,800	25,295,200
Pakistan	3,338,800	8,250,000
Turkey[b]	650,000	1,606,200
Iraq	457,000	1,129,000
Afghanistan	450,000	1,112,000
Iran	298,000	736,400
Syria	180,000	444,800
Nepal	170,300	420,700
Bangladesh	21,450	53,000
Lebanon	20,000	49,400
Jordan	150	380
Subtotal	15,822,500	39,097,400
Africa:		
Algeria	600,000	1,482,600
Morocco	294,000	726,500
Tunisia	99,000	244,600
Subtotal	993,000	2,453,700
Total	16,815,500	41,551,100
Rice		
Asia:		
India	8,639,100	21,347,200
Philippines[c]	1,752,000	4,329,200
Indonesia	1,521,000	3,758,000
Bangladesh	1,069,600	2,643,000
Vietnam (South)	835,000	2,063,300
Pakistan	643,500	1,590,000
Thailand	350,000	865,000
Malaysia	217,300	537,000
Burma	199,200	492,200
Korea (South)	187,000	462,000
Nepal	177,300	438,000
Laos	50,000	123,600
Sri Lanka	17,600	43,500
Subtotal	15,658,600	38,692,000
Latin America:		
Subtotal	429,600	1,061,400
Total	16,088,200	39,753,400

[a] Mexico, Guatemala, Taiwan, and the centrally planned economies are excluded.
[b] 1971–1972 estimate.
[c] Unofficial estimate.
Source: Dana G. Dalrymple, "Impact of the International Institutes on Crop Production" (Paper prepared for the Conference on Resource Allocation and Productivity in International Agricultural Research, Airlie House, Virginia, January 26–29, 1975), p. 22, Table 3.

With this intellectual arrogance it was easy to assume that temperate zone agricultural practices and technologies could indeed be transferred to tropical environments and societies. It was even easier to assume that the green revolution technologies had nothing to gain from the experience of the small farmer. This in fact meant that the green revolution was exclusively created on the fields and for the resources of the underdeveloped countries' rural elite. That thousands, perhaps millions of small peasants benefited briefly from the green revolution is incidental. This, after all, demonstrated for a while that the economists' pet "trickle-down" hypothesis worked.

MIRAGE IN A DESERT OF POVERTY

The green revolution establishment, including as it does powerful members of the scientific and financial elites from both the rich and the poor countries, went to unusual pains to institutionalize the mono-cropping technologies born in Mexico, thanks to the philanthropy and talent of the Rockefeller Foundation. The Rockefeller Foundation was soon joined by the Ford Foundation, and later by the World Bank, to create the arrangements for the management of scientific resources and for ready access to funds. To date the combination of organization, capital, and a concrete if unsound philosophy of agricultural development for the poor have produced what appears to be another marvel of Western ingenuity grafted in the tropics, but operated from the non-tropical board rooms of the Rockefeller and Ford foundations and of the World Bank. The substance of this global system is the international network of agricultural research centers located in the Philippines, Mexico, Colombia, Peru, Nigeria, Kenya, Ethiopia, India, Liberia, and Lebanon. In research these centers cover most of the ecological zones and foodcrops of the underdeveloped world. Their wealthy patrons have been generous with their contributions. From about $15 million in 1972 the international network is expected to spend over $60 million in 1976.

It is unlikely that $60 million will buy any more in terms of technological innovation or social good than $15 million bought in 1972. If India reflects the green revolution predicament, it can be said with certainty that the green revolution is, for all practical purposes, not merely unfinished, but over. It was more than drought that ended the green revolution in India in 1972. In fact, the short-lived spectacular spread of the HYVs in India was no more than a mirage in a desert of poverty. India has more than 100 million landless peasants, and more than 200 million rural people living in abject poverty. That the green revolution in India benefited the few and increased the number of the poor was simply axiomatic in the context of gross imbalances in the countryside. An incidence of rural violence on Christmas 1968, in the village of Kilvenmani, Tanjore District, state of Madras, South India, shows precisely the nature of those imbalances of wealth, power, and extreme poverty:

> On a long pole at the center of this desolate hamlet, a torn and faded red flag fluttered in the evening breeze. In the surrounding rice paddies, the ripened crop was wasting away. The men who were to harvest it had either fled or been jailed. On the night of December 25, 43 members of Kilvenmani's peasant families, mostly women and children, were burned to death in a thatched hut. It had been set on fire with 25 others during a bitter clash between landless farm laborers—all from castes traditionally considered untouchable—and a mob of 300 led by higher-caste land-owners . . . . Increases in production made possible by new high-yielding varieties that the Government is promoting here on the east coast with the support of the Ford Foundation have meant increases in social tension as well. Many responsible Indians are now anxiously asking whether the clash in Tanjore is a sign that rural conflict may be an inescapable part of the so-called green revolution. Wages have increased unevenly throughout the district, and the landless laborers have been agitating for even a bigger share of the new prosperity. They are now paid the equivalent of 20 cents a day, usually in kind. . . . Last year at least three cases of arson, five murders, and countless abductions and beatings were reported. The victims usually were harijan laborers. In some cases they retaliated, and landowners and their henchmen were slain.[3]

The Indian elite that does not hesitate to use violence to safeguard its land has sole access to power, wealth, and income. The vast powerless rural majority of India is landless or near landless. It has many responsibilities, but few rights to a decent survival. Precious few of the peasant farmers have the resources to command sufficient land, water, capital or credit, technical assistance or new technologies, and the institutional infrastructure and management to increase their food production and productivity. Most of them are the serfs who generate the income of the rural elite. And those who collapse into indigence join the ranks of the urban unemployed where they starve or eventually succeed in earning a meager income.

Indian agriculture, geared as it is to some degree to the needs of external or local high-income markets, is insensitive to the utilization of indigenous resources. It is based on gross land tenure inequalities at the expense of economic efficiency and of the misery of a near servile labor of millions of men, women, and children. Monopolistic practices by the rural elite and their wholesale intermediaries, bad storage, handling, and transportation facilities all but guarantee that the small farmer will remain perpetually within the confines of abject poverty.

Neither the green revolution technologies nor the green revolution establishment is responsible for India's serf rural economy. Some members of the American elite that run the international network of agricultural research centers readily admit that dramatic social changes are necessary in India and other poor countries for technology to be put to good use. They also argue correctly that the rate of agricultural technology transfer to Asia is considerably reduced by the policies of the native elites to maintain the existing inequalities in their societies. The transfer of agricultural science and technology to the underdeveloped countries depends primarily on man's relations to his social cosmos and, necessarily, on the uses of technology at his command. To be more precise, the international agricultural research network does not have much of a chance to transfer any technologies to the indigenous farmers without the cooperation, or through the institutional structure, of the national research systems.

But agricultural research and institutions in the poor countries are basically irrelevant to local needs. Foreign-educated underdeveloped country agricultural scientists prefer to work on problems that have very little to do with the conditions of their agricultural economies and especially the small-scale, household rural needs of the peasants. It is no accident then that the green revolution elite established such cordial and lasting relationships with those who had the same education and had little if any sympathy toward the peasant. This intellectual and economic congeniality inevitably led the two elites to develop technologies that slowly turned out to be more and more forbidding to the rural poor. Besides, the technological and biological components of agricultural technology make such a technology sensitive to soil, climate, wealth, and poverty. Agricultural technology transfer is an exceedingly complex technological and social process. It involves the generation, export, and adaptation of knowledge—not an easy proposition. No doubt, "very specific technical knowledge can easily be transferred but is likely to be wrong, while general results are more likely to be useful in different climates or on different crops but must first be elaborated and particularized."[4] The need for continuous adaptation and acceptance of each new technology to major or minor physical and social niches means that a lot of technology transfer never takes place.

Technology adaptation is a costly process. It is also a scientifically taxing exercise that is beyond the indigenous research capability of the underdeveloped societies. And like technology generation, technology adaptation serves the interests of its creators. That the green revolution elite developed technologies to be delivered to the agricultural sector through another elite that had nothing to do with the peasant is not insignificant. It is not surprising at all that it was the rural elite that benefited the most from knowledge financed, tested, and created by two other elites.

The transfer of agricultural science and technology to the underdeveloped countries is primarily the flow of knowledge in an environment of serious if precarious constraints. The poverty-stricken, elite-ridden rural economies of the underdeveloped world have land tenure arrangements that by their inequality determine the prevailing patterns of rural income distribution. In Latin America the rural elite is only 2 percent of the entire agricultural population of that continent. This tiny elite owns about 50 percent of all agricultural land. Its income levels are 50 to 100 times higher than those of the peasants. In Guatemala, 74.9 percent of the farmers own 11.7 percent of the land while 2.1 percent of the farms held by the elite cover 62.5 percent of the arable land. These abstract statistics say little about the meanness of daily life for the one-third to a half of the rural labor force that is perpetually unemployed.

THE HUNGER PARADOX

A labor-intensive agricultural economy based on an institutional, technological, and social arrangement favoring the peasant farmer is almost certain to end hunger and famine in many of the poor countries. These impoverished countries consume 181 kilograms per capita per year of all grains. Cereals supply about 52 percent of the calories and nearly half of the total protein of the nutritional needs of the poor. Food legumes add the much-needed amino acids that their cereals diet fails to supply. Starchy foods and ruminants are also of great dietary value to millions of people in low-income lands. To sharply focus on an individual crop in the context of the green revolution development strategy is not necessarily adequate to the needs of this complex food system. In resource-scarcity agriculture it is sound to relate water use and management to the crop mix rather than to the individual crop. Intensifying agriculture and increasing productivity demands better resource utilization. Technologies have to be developed to integrate crops and livestock, to accomodate changes in cropping patterns in irrigated and rainfed land in order to optimize income and employment and to benefit productive systems of individual foodcrops, livestock, and nonfood forage crops. Multiple cropping dominates the agriculture of the tropics where most of the world's poor live. It offers diversity. Both farmers and scientists know that diversity is security against total crop failure.

It is a paradox that hunger is not more widespread than it is. Food production reflects neither food scarcity nor changing needs. Food as a commodity overshadows the importance of food as nutrition. And land is considered more valuable as an investment rather than as productive soil. It is hardly surprising then that science is used to solve problems of political economy and not those of the world food predicament. In the tropics agriculture by necessity still feeds people. It is also in the tropics that a new agricultural science needs to be developed. But unlike the development of the green revolution, the genesis and development of a tropical agricultural scientific revolution must not divorce biology from its social and political context. Only then we can be sure to understand agriculture and transform it in a way that can serve the interest of the small peasant farmer. To maintain agricultural research within the existing social and land tenure structures of the poor countries is to reinforce those prevailing arrangements and limit the imagination and scope of agricultural science and technology to the narrowly practical. It is in this sense that the international agricultural research centers have done a disservice to science and world agriculture. Eager to meet the needs of the underdeveloped countries' elites, they failed to learn more about the complex system of economic reality and ecological necessity. With the rejection of this challenging social and scientific strategy, the agricultural institutes are full of contradictions. They are a community of pragmatism at the expense of theory. Their high-yielding foodcrop varieties are a result of a little genetics and much testing and crossing. The very affluence of the centers' technology arsenal makes it hard for the underdeveloped country scientific community to transcend the paradigm of agricultural research once transplanted into the national research system.

The urgency of the world food problem conveniently hides the fact that basic research on tropical agriculture has yet to be done. It did not drain the scientific imagination of the green revolution establishment to develop technologies based on high energy inputs, chemicals, controlled water supplies, and machinery. That, after all, was the course of development of the technologies for commercial farming throughout the Western, temperate world. But such knowledge is expensive to generate. And in the tropics it guarantees the perpetual growth of import dependence on the rich markets for scientific talent and for other less expensive inputs. But, above all, the transfer of commercial farming technologies to the underdeveloped world perpetuates an intellectual colonialism that in the long run is undermining the genesis of new centers of scientific creativity in both the poor and the rich countries. Since the purpose of agriculture must be that of feeding and providing a way of life for the majority of mankind, then its research strategy must stress whole system analysis that crosses disciplines and rejects the dichotomy of fundamental versus applied research. That this is crucial for the poor countries needs no evidence. They have few, badly trained agricultural scientists. No crash program could possibly change the poverty of their agriculture. Instead, what these countries must do is to restructure their research so that they can effectively mobilize their total intellectual resources. They must also end the precarious imbalance between their tiny elites of wealth, income, and power and the great majorities of poverty, impoverishment, and impotence.

FEAR IN THE COUNTRYSIDE

The peasant farmer is the backbone and victim of both the economy and poverty in the underdeveloped countries. For some years now this small farmer has found an eloquent defender in the courts of the rich in Robert McNamara of the World Bank:

> What many of us sometimes forget is that just because a man is poor does not mean that he is naive. The truth is that millions of small farmers— even without elaborate inputs—could increase their productivity measurably if they could be given but one simple assurance: that at harvest time they would be able to sell their additional production at a rewarding price. Moreover, the small farmer is almost always discriminated against by public institutions that tend to favor the larger and more prosperous producers. It is the larger farmer who typically enjoys easy access to public credit, research, water allocations, and scarce supplies of petroleum, pesticides, and fertilizer. And it is the smaller farmer who is left to wait endlessly for the public services he needs far more urgently, but only too rarely receives.[5]

Other members of the green revolution elite share McNamara's sympathy for the small farmer. They argue that the fate of the small peasant farmer in the poor countries is becoming "an important conscious priority" in the international agricultural research system. Technologies are designed exclusively to benefit the poor farmer. But the reality in one of the network institutes, the International Center for Tropical Agriculture (CIAT) in Colombia, does not in the least reflect concern for the small farmer. CIAT, which received its first funding in 1969, serves the agroclimatic area of the rainfed and irrigated tropics. But like its host country's institutions, CIAT functions within the Colombian context of fear and neglect for the small farmer. Located on a lush farm of Palmira, "the agricultural capital of Colombia," CIAT does not have much to offer to Colombian or international tropical agricultural development. Its rice technologies did reach the prosperous rice producers. Its beef and bean programs have had no impact yet. And while CIAT's cassava technology brought "spectacular results" in controlled experimental plots, it still has to be transferred to the farmers. The promising swine nutrition technology is slowly being dismantled and the equally promising small farmer project was recently abolished.

That CIAT abolished the only program it had developed with the thrust to transfer technologies to the small farmer is certainly a telling point between rhetoric on the welfare of the small holders and actual neglect for rural poverty. Working as they do within the confines of a reward-penalty system, the international agricultural research institutes are mainly concerned with increasing the national yields of their commodity crops. They are technology-producing factories that do not dare to help the small farmer, lest better living standards for millions of rural poor upset the native elites' monopoly of power and wealth. That is exactly what happened with CIAT and its small farm systems. The scientists in the CIAT small farmer project made no effort to hide the fact that their impact would have radical social consequences in the rural communities covered by the small farm systems. Such talk was apparently uncongenial to the CIAT board of trustees: early in 1975 the board abolished the project. Meanwhile, the wave of rural violence continues in Colombia. The food situation continues to be precarious. And the pathology of land distribution continues to threaten the very existence of the Indians and to spark peasant invasion of the land of other peasants and of the land of the rich.

The green revolution will remain unfinished as long as it bypasses the small peasant farmer. The poor peasant of the underdeveloped countries is master of local agricultural technologies that have the wisdom of centuries of evolution and development. The green revolution can once more become green by using the best of Western technology to better and not to replace existing food and agricultural practices and technologies. The earth can feed all of its inhabitants. The fact that there are malnourished or starving people mirrors bad economics, bad distribution of resources, and social injustice. The small farmer produces most of the food in the underdeveloped regions of the world. This is not because he has enough land but because he makes his tiny plot productive. In Colombia, with only one-fourth of the cropland under his plow, the small farmer generates two-thirds of all output in the agricultural sector. And in the northeast region of Brazil the small farmer produces 14 times as much per hectare than the large farmer. Yet the small farmer is outside of the political economies of the underdeveloped countries. He is also beyond the reach of technology transfer and development, with the result that new technologies fail to

Table C–3. Imbalance Between Man and Land in Colombia, 1960 and 1970 (Rapid Disappearance of the Small Farmer)

Hectares	Number of Farms				Total Area in Hectares			
	1960	Percent	1970	Percent	1960	Percent	1970	Percent
0–10	925,750	76.52	821,854	72.10	2,303,725	8.45	2,176,246	6.13
10–50	201,020	16.60	217,236	19.10	4,210,777	15.45	4,689,599	14.94
50–200	62,307	5.15	75,670	6.64	5,676,623	20.84	6,863,650	21.90
200–1000	17,834	1.47	21,420	1.87	6,725,083	24.70	8,054,244	25.66
1000–2500	1,975	0.16	2,299	0.20	2,808,210	10.30	3,334,201	10.62
+2500	786	0.06	1,023	0.08	5,513,409	20.24	6,264,381	19.96
Total	1,209,672		1,139,502		27,237,827		31,382,321	

Source: Rafael T. Posada, "La situacion del pequeño agricultor en Colombia" (Paper, Programa de Sistemas para Pequeños Agricultores, Centro Internacional de Agricultura Tropical, September 1974), p. 4, Table 1.

Table C–4.   Measures of Land and Capital Productivity by Farm Size in the Northeast Region of Brazil, 1972 (High Productivity of the Small Farmer)

Property Size	Properties	Total Value of Production		Value of Production Sold	
			Percent of Property		Percent of Property
Hectares	Number	Cr$/ha	Value[a]	Cr$/ha	Value[a]
Less than 1	12,228	700	42.6	325	19.8
1–2	41,201	465	44.7	224	21.5
2–5	112,148	326	44.8	168	23.1
5–10	108,456	226	[b]	122	[b]
10–25	165,899	158	41.0	93	24.2
25–50	113,541	112	37.3	69	23.0
50–100	89,770	92	37.4	61	24.8
100–200	59,329	72	32.6	51	23.1
200–500	39,356	64	33.0	46	23.7
500–1000	12,187	59	30.9	45	23.6
1000–2000	5,168	50	27.7	39	21.4
2000 and above	2,815	48	31.8	36	23.8
Total	762,188	75	34.9	51	23.7

[a] The residence and recreational facilities value is excluded.

[b] Data inconsistencies.

In 1970, 62.6 percent of the "economically active population" of northeast Brazil was engaged in agriculture. Most of the land of this region is in the hands of the rural elite. Farms of more than 200 hectares in size represent only 3 percent of total farm units but cover 58 percent of the available cropland. With this extreme concentration of land by the privileged few it is not surprising that the many must make a living on "extraordinarily small units." Northeast Brazil suffers from "extremely low rural incomes and massive underemployment." In the context of these gross inequalities the small farmers still manage to have commercialization rates equal to or higher than the larger farmers.

Source: D. Young and K. Corum, "Differential Impact of Selected Agricultural Policies According to Farm Size: A Case Study of a County in the 'Agreste' Region of Northeast Brazil" (Paper, EMBRAPA/USAID Project, Recife, Pe., Brazil, May 1975), pp. 2, 17–18, Table 7.

be tailored to local conditions. Only by redressing this imbalance will the poor countries succeed in feeding their rapidly increasing populations. It is not easy to exaggerate their food predicament. It remains precarious.

The most formidable constraint the poor countries face in their efforts to eliminate hunger and redress their poverty is poverty itself. There are some disparities among the rich countries. But such disparities are certainly modest compared to the widening gulf between them and the underdeveloped countries. The low-income nonoil nations must wait for an entire decade for a $3 increase in their real per

**Table C–5. Trends in per Capita Food Production
(1961–1965 Average = 100)**

	Latin America	Far East[a]	Near East[b]	Africa[c]
1968	99	100	104	100
1969	102	102	104	102
1970	102	105	103	101
1971	100	102	101	102
1972	97	97	106	101

[a] Excluding China and Japan.
[b] Excluding Israel.
[c] Excluding South Africa.
Source: United Nations, Food and Agriculture Organization, *The State of Food and Agriculture 1973* (Rome: FAO, 1973), pp. 182–188.

capita incomes, while their trade deficit is running into billions of dollars.

Equally crippling to the development of the poor countries is their rural elites and the contempt these landowning minorities feel for their peasant majorities. The massive exodus of the rural population of the underdeveloped countries from agriculture to the cities reflects the desperate effort of the peasants to escape the crushing poverty of their social and physical environment. These peasants have vastly inferior basic facilities like water and health care. Their children can for the most part aspire to no more than two years of elementary schooling. Their levels of living have changed very little. For centuries they have lived in the mountain regions and the flatlands. Some are small landowners, some are sharecroppers, and some work in the rich farmland of the rural elite. When a family collapses into indigence it breaks up, joining gangs of rural guerillas or becoming urban beggars, prostitutes, and thieves. The margin of survival for both the poor and the indigent is narrow. And yet they maintain their fragile, makeshift economy through hard labor, migration, violence, and the stability of their family structure.

Meanwhile, institutionalized land tenure inequalities permit the small rural elite to use the landless agricultural workers as labor in return for a wage of perpetual poverty. The landholder has both state and local resources at his command. Everything functions at his discretion and good will. His patronage is essential for social services. And the business institutions operate largely for his convenience. He not only controls the resources of agricultural investment but is the chief beneficiary of technical assistance and rural infrastructure. As a large landowner he has unlimited access to institutional credit.

**Table C–6. Income and Investment Levels 1970–1980 for Developed and Developing Countries[a]
(In 1970 Dollars)**

Country Group	1975 Population (in millions)	GNP per Capita 1970	GNP per Capita 1980	GNP Growth Rate Per Capita Per Annum (percent)	Estimated Investment Per Capita Per Annum — Domestic Savings	Estimated Investment Per Capita Per Annum — External Capital Inflow	Estimated Investment Per Capita Per Annum — Total
I. Low-income Countries (Under $200 per capita per annum)	1,000	$ 105	$ 108	0.2	$ 14	$ 2	$ 16
II. Middle-income Countries (over $200 per capita per annum)	725	$ 410	$ 540	2.8	$ 75	$ 10	$ 85
III. OECD Countries	675	$3,100	$4,000	2.6	$850	$–15	$835

[a]Excludes centrally planned economies and OPEC. Assumes Case I rates of growth for the developing countries 1976–1980.
Source: Robert S. McNamara, *Address to the Board of Governors* (Washington, D.C.: International Bank for Reconstruction and Development, September 1, 1975), p. 7.

MORE LAND, TECHNICAL ASSISTANCE, AND CREDIT

In most of the poor countries a good proportion of the labor force is tied up in producing just enough food for local consumption. The high man-land ratio and the extremely low yields per acre result in disastrously low real incomes for most of the rural people. In addition to strengthening existing social inequalities this low productivity certainly perpetuates the serious nutritional deficiencies of the poor. Appropriate advanced technologies in an appropriate land tenure context can correct the imbalances of subsistence agriculture, supported as it is by the underutilization of the huge rural labor force. New technologies need not be labor-saving. Technological reforms and improvements demand more work in preparing the soil, sowing, weeding, and harvesting. Sharecropping undermines technology transfer and its sustained and efficient utilization. Sharecropping is also inimical to resource allocation for the very advances in agriculture technology that alone can raise labor utilization and yields. But most of the rural people have no surplus income or even enough land to permit a reasonable increase in agricultural investment. And those who own most of the rural income and land have shown neither the interest to better their farms and raise their productivity nor the capacity to commit themselves seriously to farming. Instead, the landowning elites of the underdeveloped countries spend their profits on luxury consumption or urban investment, or simply send them out of the country.

The effort of the West to make the big landowner the main food provider of the underdeveloped countries has clearly failed. Western institutions, be they international agricultural research centers, multinational corporations, or technical assistance agencies, are showing signs of ossification with decaying ideas and development priorities. Bypassing as they do the vast rural majorities of the poor countries, they feel comfortable with elite-consumed technologies, elite-inspired economic thinking, and elite-controlled social and political structures. They have sought to fuel an agricultural revolution in the poor countries by a technology that is for the most part inappropriate to the needs of the small tropical farmer and in the context of increasing inequalities in the agricultural sector. Some members of the Western elite like to talk about the rural poor and the global food problem. But so far they have not managed to turn their theoretical and often humanitarian speculations into concrete action. Multinational corporation executives attend and finance conferences to justify their "social responsibility." And yet they are not even willing to encourage, much less support, research to explore ways for the corporations to help the poor farmer break the vicious chains of poverty. But while the rich country elites can afford to maintain their "neutrality" to the brutal realities of backwardness, the poor country elites must be aware that underdevelopment is slowly eroding the ecological as well as the human environment of their own countries. It is pointless to hold tenaciously to a largely undermined colonial legacy of keeping the majority of the population at a state of perpetual poverty and malnutrition.

If not human kindness, at least technology and energy have made slavery obsolete. It is reasonable to assume that enough citizens of the poor countries will have the courage to face the fundamental fact that the small farmers, constituting as they do the most productive sector of their societies, deserve not contempt but more land, technical assistance, and credit. In short, the small farmers deserve to be brought into the realms of political power and technology. Hunger and malnutrition are the grim center of the world food problem. But it is poverty and social injustice that provide the soil for the growth of hunger and malnutrition. Land reform, bringing social and economic justice and contributing to higher productivity, is a critical development priority for the underdeveloped countries. The contradiction between the millions of landless peasants and the tiny minority that owns most of the land is bound to feed the sparks of violent revolution unless land reform and technologies of inequality reduction bring justice to the precarious rural environment.

APPROACHING THE GREY SPRING AND RAINY SEASON

The Greek poet Hesiod lived around the seventh century B.C. In his *Works and Days* he gave practical advice on divination, astronomy, navigation, housekeeping, and agriculture. For our study the importance of Hesiod is to be found in the fact that 27 centuries ago he exhorted men to work and to be just to each other. He saw heroism and dignity in the farmer's long and silent struggle with the "black" earth and with the elements. He said:

> Take note, when you hear the voice of the crane, who cries every year from high in the clouds; she gives the signal for ploughing, and points to the season of rainy winter; she pains the heart of the man with no oxen. . . . As soon as the time for ploughing is announced to men, then set out quickly, you and your slaves, in dry and in wet, to plough in the season for ploughing, hurrying out very early in the morning, so that your fields will be full. Plough in the spring; but fallow land just broken

Figure C-1. The World Food Problem

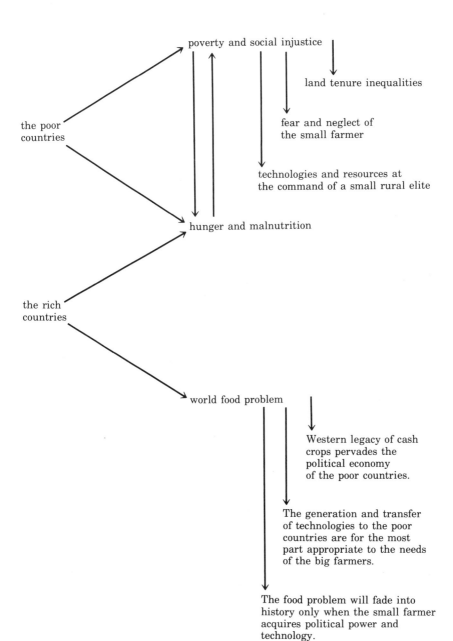

up in the summer will not disappoint your hopes. Sow the fallow land when the soil is still light; fallow land will protect you from harm, will comfort your children. When you first begin ploughing, pray to Zeus of the Earth and to pure Demeter, to make Demeter's holy grain ripe and thick as you hold the end of the plough-handle in your hand and bring your stick down on the back of the oxen while they pull the pole-bar by the yoke-straps. And let a young slave follow behind with a mattock and make it difficult for the birds by covering the seed well; for the habit of good management is the best there is for mortal men, and that of bad management is the worst. If you do this, your corn-ears will bow to the ground in abundance, if the Olympian later grants a good outcome, and you will drive the cobwebs from your storage vessels. And I expect you will be glad when you live off the things that are stored in your house. In plenty will you reach grey springtime, and you will not turn to others for help, but another will have need of you. But if you plough the holy earth at the solstice, you will grasp a thin [crop] with your hand as you reap, stooping down and, far from rejoicing, binding the sheaves cross-wise, covered with dust; you will bring it all back in a basket and few will admire you. But the thoughts of aegis-bearing Zeus are different at different times, and it is hard for mortal men to understand them. Should you plough late, this may be the remedy: when the cuckoo first cuckoos in the leaves of the oak and delights men over the boundless earth, if Zeus then sends rain on the third day and does not cease—not rising above the ox's hoof nor falling short of it—in this way the late plougher would catch up with the early. Keep all this well in your mind, and do not let the approach of grey spring and the rainy season escape you.[6]

In the non-Western world of the late twentieth century agriculture differs little from the agriculture of Hesiod's age. The farmer of the poor countries has the capacity and potential to improve his methods and produce more food. The traditional farmer's ability to work hard and to make efficient use of his limited resources can facilitate the transfer of agricultural science and technology when such knowledge can be adapted to enrich his material life rather than posing a threat to his very existence. New technologies expanded the potential of the traditional farmer for agricultural modernization. And yet this farmer has not benefited fully from the rich resources of Western scientific and technological knowledge. This is because within his own country he has little if any control of the agricultural resources, be they technological or material. The key to agricultural modernization is no less than sustained reform of the entire institutional structure so that the peasant farmer can live and work in an environment congenial to opportunity for betterment. The rich countries can help the rural majorities of the poor countries by developing appropriate technologies for the tropical and subtropical environments. They can also use their technologies and power to insist that the underdeveloped country elites direct their development goals to benefit their vast rural majorities. In most of the underdeveloped countries inequality is increasingly gross and harsh. This trend can be reversed if the transfer and generation of technological innovation complements rather than replaces profound and sustained social change.

POLITICAL POWER AND TECHNOLOGY

It is unfortunate that at this critical juncture in history funds allocated to agricultural research are decreasing. This shows that feeding the poor is not exactly a high priority, here or elsewhere. And this savage attitude is especially prevalent among the elites who govern the world's poor. These elites preside over more than two billion of the planet's population. Seventy percent of this humanity lives in rural areas. These hundreds of millions live or barely survive "on the margin of life, living under conditions so degraded by disease, illiteracy, malnutrition, and squalor as to be denied the basic human necessities."[7] On the basis of this staggering fact it seems that now more than ever science must help the poor small peasant farmer. Development has enriched only the urban middle class and the rural elite. As for the vast majority of the people of these countries, the only thing that can be said with certainty is that they are neither organized nor well informed to know what their interests are.[8]

Continuously evolving technologies could in principle be used to solve problems of rural inequality. But with the exception of Taiwan this has not happened, because technology at present is inadequate. The reason must also be sought in inappropriate institutions and poor policy. Again, the point here is not that those who govern are ignorant, but that those who are governed have no power.[9] Technical assistance and aid flowing to countries with social structures that exclude the poor and powerless from the political process have for the most part been "irrelevant or negative for development."[10] This does not mean that all efforts to help the poor countries modernize ought to be abandoned. Experience shows that technical assistance does often stimulate economic growth with its allocation of technology, skills, and capital. It may also spread social justice as it makes it possible for more people to taste the fruits of technology and knowledge:

> But we would be naive or hypocritical to believe that helping governments implement conservative development strategies of technological modernization and economic growth, which do not consider the welfare and participation of the rural poor as real high-priority goals, will in

some miraculous fashion directly benefit more than a very few of the poverty-stricken small farmers and landless labourers. These are the groups, however, that will make up most of the rural population in the developing countries for a long time to come, and which have little possibility of benefiting from development within traditional social structures. In fact, their immediate prospects are for continued poverty and repression in a large part of the world.[11]

It is no accident that agriculture was the mother of the green revolution. Agriculture "was the first science—the mother of sciences; it remains the science which makes human life possible; and it may well be that, before the century is over, the success or failure of Science as a whole will be judged by the success or failure of agriculture."[12] But the green revolution must abandon its misdirected priority of serving best those who need its technologies least. It must put its considerable resources at the disposal of the peasant throughout the world. It can then become the first global revolution in human history. Its new technologies will feed the poor. They will also reorder human priorities for the benefit of mankind. They will water the seeds for a better harvest. This harvest must see to the elimination of hunger. At the same time *it must create the global foundations for the eradication of social inequality in the underdeveloped countries.* Only then will the poor peasant farmer be able to utilize new technologies. He and the rest of the world's poor can then join the human family with a sense of commitment to limiting their rapidly increasing numbers and getting the benefits of technological civilization.

It has been suggested that "increased production of basic food crops everywhere has at last been accepted as the primary solution to the world food problem."[13] Technologically, this may in fact be a plausible hypothesis. But the world food problem and the international transfer of agricultural technology involve much more than land, water, and technology. They are primarily questions of power. As long as the elites of the underdeveloped countries control knowledge and the resources of agriculture, there is very little hope that the small farmer will manage to alter his environment of scarcity and poverty without resorting to violence. Bloody peasant revolutions can be averted only if there is an immediate and sustained transfer of resources from those who control the land to those who work it. But this is not likely to happen. It appears, then, that the only alternative to the preservation of fear in the world countryside is for the world's peasants to overthrow the elite-supported institutions of backwardness. Backwardness in the underdeveloped countries deprives the poor of the opportunity for a better life. It chains millions of people to a demoralizing and humiliating slavery. Those chains must be broken. And the United States will be within its own traditions of liberty and equality to direct and structure its considerable resources to lead and facilitate peasant social revolutions wherever rural majorities are oppressed, especially in Latin America. Both the United States' involvement and the inevitable social revolutions in the poor countries are likely to be violent. Such violence can be mitigated and perhaps avoided were U.S. policy to evolve in the following way:

1. Technologies alone will do very little to correct the abysmal inequalities governing the food and political economies of the poor countries. However, when these technologies are intermediate and/or appropriate they induce change by increasing the productivity of the small farmer. With the enactment of the 1975 International Development and Food Assistance Act the U.S. Congress committed the United States to side with the world's poor. This means that all U.S. technical assistance must be designed to be appropriate and *to reach* the small rural worker and farmer.

2. What is suggested here is no less than a veritable renaissance in appropriate agrarian technologies. Such a technological revival in the United States' political and educational institutions must utilize the fact that the small farmer is a considerable intellectual resource. It would be both challenging and timely for the U.S. Congress to direct American resources to better rather than replace the existing food and agricultural practices in the small farm sector at home and in the underdeveloped countries. Congress will then have the opportunity to revolutionize the American-funded international agricultural research centers by transforming them into resource transfer mechanisms to serve the poor farmer. Congress must make certain that the Agency for International Development (AID) and other U.S. technical assistance institutions transfer to the poor countries only those technologies that do in fact redistribute income at the small farm agricultural sector. It is equally important that Congress monitor such resource transfers. A bipartisan congressional committee can also evaluate the need for massive and sustained U.S. assistance to the U.S. small producer and to the resource-scarcity agriculture of those countries willing to help their own poor. In short, the U.S. Congress must declare, in no uncertain terms, that henceforth no country that penalizes its own rural majority can expect to preserve U.S. assistance and friendship.

The implementation of this proposed policy will have a sobering effect on those who terrorize the poor in the countryside. It is equally

certain to undermine the spread of communist and *latifundia* dictator-
ships in the underdeveloped world. At the same time this policy will
have the support of the U.S. people with the most lasting tradition of
helping others in need. It will restore confidence here and abroad that
the United States is firmly upholding its revolutionary ideas of democratic institutions and decency.

Ours is also an appropriate period in human history for the out-
break of an intellectual revolution in men's minds, a redefinition of
development in an effort to reunite ethics and politics. In such a
context science can truly serve mankind. It is a serious and disturbing
proposition to consider that man, 24 centuries after the collapse of the
Greek city-state, has not yet learned that the Greeks, despite their
philosophy and science, lost their freedom precisely because they failed
to treat each other as members of one family. And they resorted to civil
wars despite Socrates, Plato, and Aristotle, and despite the fact that
they called every non-Greek a barbarian. Today we have no barbarians
left. But we are all in a sense barbarians. There is no other way to
explain the existence of nuclear weapons, the world food problem, etc.
This does not mean that man has lost the battle for a decent, humane
existence. On the contrary, we have the brains and the hearts to follow
a global social policy. The poor peasant farmer needs a chance to better
his yields and standard of living. The question we face is whether we,
mankind, can also take the chance we already have to become more
ethical and humane:

> Snakes can grow only by bursting their skin. Molting has to be a painful
> process, and should it fail the snake would die. Mankind also grows by
> now and then bursting its outgrown skin of antiquated ideas, thinking
> and institutions. . . . We either adapt to the new situation, revamp our
> thinking and human relations, exchange our outdated ideas of glory,
> force, domination and exploitation for mutual understanding, respect
> help and collaboration, or else perish. At present we are heading for
> extinction and who will shed tears for us? Who regrets the dinosaur?[14]

Notes

INTRODUCTION

1. Cornelius Walford, *The Famines of the World: Past and Present* (London: Edward Stanford, 1879), p. 7.

2. Ibid., pp. 12–14.

3. "Plans for the Future—A Statement by the Trustees of the Rockefeller Foundation, September 20, 1963," in Carroll P. Streeter, *A Report from the Rockefeller Foundation: A Partnership to Improve Food Production in India* (New York: The Rockefeller Foundation, 1969), p. iv.

4. Nevin S. Scrimshaw, "Food," *Scientific American*, 209, no. 3 (September 1963), 73.

5. Lyle P. Schertz, "World Food: Prices and the Poor," *Foreign Affairs*, 52, no. 3 (April 1974), 511.

6. Cattle around the world consume enough food to feed 8.7 billion people: Georg Borgstrom cited by Boyce Rensberger, "World Food Crises: Basic Ways of Life Face Upheaval," *The New York Times*, November 5, 1974, p. 14.

7. Schertz, pp. 512–513, 519.

8. National Science Foundation, National Science Board, *Patterns and Perspectives in Environmental Science* (Washington, D.C.: U.S. Government Printing Office, 1972), p. 391.

9. Peter Grose, "On Energy Policy," *The New York Times*, December 17, 1974, p. 37.

10. Roger Revelle, Lecture, Natural Sciences 118, November 18, 1974, Harvard University. The source of the quotation was one of Revelle's Indian friends. Revelle's lectures have guided my thoughts on natural resources, energy, food, and the environment.

11. René Dubos' *Man Adapting* is a work of scholarship and of original ideas on human ecology. Dubos brings together the sciences and the

humanities with the result that *Man Adapting* is a full, rich book. It shows the challenge and creativity that was needed in the evolution of man. Its treatment of food, medicine, health, air pollution, population, and the environment is provocative enough to help us re-examine our assumptions about man's role in the natural and social cosmos. In reading Dubos' book there is a subtle but cogent sense of uneasiness about the quality of human life, be that in terms of environmental pollution or misdirected medical research.

12. Adamantios Koraes, "Report on the Present State of Civilization in Greece," in *Nationalism in Asia and Africa*, edited by Elie Kedourie (Cleveland: The World Publishing Company, 1970), p. 185.

13. John E. Sawyer, "As the World Turns," *The New York Times*, December 30, 1974, p. 23.

14. Kenneth W. Thompson, "The Green Revolution," *The Center Magazine*, VI, no. 6 (November-December 1973), 59.

15. Some writers have argued that technological society emerged in the form of an undifferentiated conjuncture of techniques. This view has been forcefully expounded by the French social philosopher Jacques Ellul in his *La Technique*, translated into English as *The Technological Society* (New York: Random House, 1964). A similar emphasis upon the erosion of moral values brought about by the dominance of technique is to be found in Theodore Roszak's *Where the Wasteland Ends: Politics and Transcendence in Postindustrial Society* (Garden City, N.Y.: Anchor Books, 1973). For Roszak, society has become technocratic and technocracy has become teratoid. Both Ellul and Roszak believe that the technological-technocratic civilization of our times is slowly but steadily dehumanizing mankind. Whatever the merits of their thesis, they reflect social philosophies in response to our technological civilization. And it is this technological civilization that is flowing to the poor nations for development.

16. M. Taghi Farvar and John P. Milton, eds., *The Careless Technology: Ecology and International Development* (New York: The Natural History Press, 1972), pp. 159–367; Barbara Ward and René Dubos, *Only One Earth: The Care and Maintenance of a Small Planet* (New York: W.W. Norton, 1972), pp. 158–165; Landing Savané, "Problems of Scientific and Technological Development in Black Africa," *Impact of Science on Society*, XXIII, no. 2 (April-June 1973), 90.

17. John McHale, *The Future of the Future* (New York: Ballantine Books, 1971), pp. 14–15.

18. Charles R. Walker, ed., *Modern Technology and Civilization* (New York: McGraw-Hill, 1962), p. 380. I am indebted to Professor Everett Mendelsohn of Harvard University for the theses on the countercultural role and social construction of science.

19. Edward Atiyah, *An Arab Tells His Story: A Study in Loyalties* (London: John Murray, 1949), pp. 31–32.

20. *Finance and Development*, IX, no. 2 (June 1972), 62.

21. Hasan Ozbekhan, *Technology and Man's Future* (Santa Monica: System Development Corporation, 1966), p. 29.

22. Gunnar Myrdal, *Against the Stream: Critical Essays on Economics* (New York: Vintage Books, 1975), pp. 71–84.

23. Robert S. McNamara, "Greening the Landscape," *Saturday Review/World*, December 14, 1974, pp. 36, 108.

24. Food and Agriculture Organization of the United Nations, *The State of Food and Agriculture 1972* (Rome, 1972), p. 143.

25. Werner Kiene (Ford Foundation), interview, New York, February 19, 1975.

26. Richard Levins (Department of Biology, University of Chicago), letter addressed to this author, Chicago, February 11, 1975. In the fall of 1975 Levins joined the Department of Population Sciences, Harvard University.

27. Myrdal, p. 190.

28. Solon L. Barraclough, "Politics First," *Ceres*, 7, no. 5 (September-October 1974), 28.

29. In a July 1, 1975, editorial essay appropriately entitled "The hungry still wait," *The Boston Evening Globe* registered the diminishing world concern on the food problem: "The sense of urgency that accompanied the world food crisis a year ago seems to have all but disappeared and there is a grave danger that the world may not make a serious and sustained effort to deal with the problem." (p. 12.)

30. A classic eulogy of the green revolution was written by Robert Katz, *A Giant in the Earth* (New York: Stein and Day, 1973).

31. Bruno Kreisky, "Strengthening the 'Fourth World,'" *The New York Times*, August 16, 1975, p. 19.

32. Moises Behar, director, Institute of Nutrition of Central America and Panama, and chief of the nutrition unit of WHO, quoted in *The New York Times*, August 26, 1975, p. 9.

33. Roger Revelle, "Food and Population," *Scientific American*, 231, no. 3 (September 1974), 169.

34. Roger Revelle, "The Scientist and the Politician," *Science*, 187, (March 21, 1975), 1104.

35. Letter to the Editor, *The New York Times*, July 31, 1975, p. 26.

36. William Foote Whyte, "Organizing for Agricultural Development" (Paper, New York State School of Industrial and Labor Relations, Cornell University, October 15, 1974), p. 44.

37. Roger Revelle, "On Technical Assistance and Bilateral Aid," *Bulletin of the Atomic Scientists*, XXIV, no. 3 (March 1968), 17.

38. Alden J. Stevenson, "The Arithmetic of Hunger," *Jesuit Missions*, 41 (July-August 1967), 7.

CHAPTER 1

1. Quoted in George Martelli, *Léopold to Lumumba: A History of the Belgian Congo 1877–1960* (London: Chapman and Hall, 1962), p. 19.

2. Montague Yudelman, *Africans on the Land* (Cambridge, Mass.: Harvard University Press, 1964), p. 39.

3. *East Africa Royal Commission, 1953–1955 Report* (London: H.M.S.O., 1955), p. 23.

4. W.K. Hancock, *Survey of British Commonwealth Affairs*, Vol II: *Problems of Economic Policy, 1918–1939* (London: Oxford University Press, 1942), pt. II, p. 101.

5. V.S. Naipaul, "Argentina: The Brothels Behind the Graveyard," *The New York Review*, September 19, 1974, p. 13.

6. Arminius Vambery, *Western Culture in Eastern Lands* (London: J. Murray, 1906), pp. 1–4.

7. Edward Atiyah, *An Arab Tells his Story: A Study in Loyalties* (London: John Murray, 1949), p. 29.

8. William Woodruff, *Impact of Western Man: A Study of Europe's Role in the World Economy 1750–1960* (New York: St. Martin's Press, 1967), pp. 167–174.

9. *Official Year Book of the Colony of Southern Rhodesia: Statistics and General Information* (Salisbury: Art Printing and Publishing Works, 1924), p. 66.

10. Philip Mason, *The Birth of a Dilemma: The Conquest and Settlement of Rhodesia* (London: Oxford University Press, 1958), pp. 100–101.

11. C.C. Wrigley, *Crops and Wealth in Uganda* (Kampala, Uganda: East African Institute of Social Research, 1959), pp. 64–65.

12. Ibid., pp. 56–57.

13. Woodruff, p. 185.

14. Akhter Hameed Khan, "The Comilla Projects—A Personal Account" (Paper prepared for Development from Below, Field Trip/Workshop, Addis Ababa, Ethiopia, October 12–20, 1973), p. 5.

15. R.I. Crane, "India: A Study of the Impact of Western Civilization," *Social Education*, XV (December 1951), 365–369.

16. Edward Baines, *History of the Cotton Manufacture in Great Britain* (London: H. Fisher, R. Fisher, and P. Jackson, 1835), p. 56.

17. Shri Dharampal, ed., *Indian Science and Technology in the Eighteenth Century: Some Contemporary Accounts* (New Delhi: Impex India, 1971), pp. 180–199.

18. Ibid., p. 183.

19. P. Spear, *India, Pakistan, and the West* (London: Home University Library, 1958), pp. 132–133.

20. Dharampal, p. 182.

21. Abul-Fazl M. Abdur-Rahman, quoted in Cornelius Walford, *Famines of the World: Past and Present* (London: Edward Stanford, 1879), pp. 103–104.

22. C.R. Boxer, "Sakoku, or the Closed Country, 1640–1854," *History Today*, VII (February 1957), 85.

23. Quoted in F. Whyte, *China and Foreign Powers* (London: Oxford University Press, 1927), p. 38.

24. K.M. Panikkar, *Asia and Western Dominance* (London: G. Allen, 1953), pp. 205–206.

25. S. Teng and J.K. Fairbank, *China's Response to the West: A Documentary Survey, 1839–1923* (Cambridge, Mass.: Harvard University Press, 1954), pp. 126–127.

26. George Sansom, *A History of Japan 1615–1867* (Stanford: Stanford University Press, 1963), p. 99.

27. Thomas C. Smith, "The Japanese Village in the Seventeenth Century," *Journal of Economic History*, XII, no. 1 (Winter 1952), 13.

28. Thomas C. Smith, *Political Change and Industrial Development in Japan: Government Enterprise, 1868–1880* (Stanford: Stanford University Press, 1955), pp. 17–18.

29. Michael Cooper, ed., *They Came to Japan: An Anthology of European Reports on Japan, 1543–1640* (Berkeley: University of California Press, 1965), p. 7.

30. Yujiro Hayami, "Innovations in the Fertilizer Industry and Agricultural Development: The Japanese Experience," *Journal of Farm Economics*, 49, no. 2 (May 1967), 403–412.

31. Kazushi Ohkawa and Henry Rosovsky, "The Role of Agriculture in Modern Japanese Economic Development," in *Agriculture in Economic Development*, edited by Carl K. Eicher and Lawrence Witt (New York: McGraw-Hill, 1964), pp. 52–53.

32. Ibid., pp. 50–51.

33. Kusum Nair, *The Lonely Furrow: Farming in the United States, Japan and India* (Ann Arbor: University of Michigan Press, 1969), p. 115.

34. D.V. Reddy, *Farmers Behavioral Change Through the Strategy of Agricultural Development in India* (New Delhi: Offset Press, Directorate of Extension, Ministry of Food, Agriculture, CD and Cooperation, [late 1960s]), p. 1.

35. In Lester R. Brown, "The Social Impact of the Green Revolution," *International Conciliation*, no. 581 (January 1971), p. 47.

36. Reddy, pp. 11, 13.

37. Ibid., p. 17.

38. Ibid., p. 20.

39. Nair, p. 209.

40. Ibid., p. 216.

41. Ibid., pp. 217–219.

42. W. David Hopper, "The Economic Organization of a Village in North Central India" (Ph.D thesis, Cornell University, 1957), quoted in Theodore W. Schultz, *Transforming Traditional Agriculture* (New Haven: Yale University Press, 1964), p. 45.

43. Hayami, pp. 403–412.

44. Ohkawa and Rosovsky, pp. 46–47.

45. M.C. Chaturvedi, "Poverty, Population and Technology: A Sketch of Population-Resource Development Dilemma in India" (Paper, Harvard Center for Population Studies, Cambridge, Mass., 1974), p. 7. Chaturvedi is a senior professor, Indian Institute of Technology, New Delhi, India.

46. Ibid., pp. 1–4.

47. Alden J. Stevenson, "The Arithmetic of Hunger," *Jesuit Missions*, 41 (July-August 1967), 9.

48. Walford, p. 90.

49. Roger Revelle, Lecture, Natural Sciences 118, November 25, 1974, Harvard University.

CHAPTER 2

1. William Woodruff, *Impact of Western Man: A Study of Europe's Role in the World Economy 1750–1960* (New York: St. Martin's Press, 1967), p. 198.

2. Zvi Griliches, "Research Costs and Social Returns: Hybrid Corn and Related Innovations," in *Agriculture in Economic Development*, edited by Carl K. Eicher and Lawrence Witt (New York: McGraw-Hill, 1964), p. 370.

3. Ibid., pp. 370, 380.

4. Kenneth W. Thompson, "The Green Revolution," *The Center Magazine*, VI, no. 6 (November-December 1973), 63.

5. Norman E. Borlaug, "The Impact of Agricultural Research on Mexican Wheat Production," *Transactions of the New York Academy of Sciences*, ser. II, XX, no. 3 (January 1958), 288–291.

6. Quoted in Elvin C. Stakman et al., *Campaigns Against Hunger* (Cambridge, Mass.: Harvard University Press, 1967), p. 12.

7. Quoted in Ibid., p. 14.

8. Norman E. Borlaug, "The Green Revolution: For Bread and Peace," *Bulletin of the Atomic Scientists*, XXVII, no. 6 (June 1971), 7.

9. Roger Revelle, interview, Harvard Center for Population Studies, October 22, 1974.

10. Borlaug, p. 9.

11. Stakman et al., p. 210.

12. This author interviewed most of the members of this elite. Specific reference to an idea will be given when it represents the views of an individual only and does not necessarily reflect those of the elite as a whole. Data from written sources will be documented. The definition of this elite is purposely narrow for reasons of brevity and analysis. By elite no more is meant than the skilled or privileged members of a given class.

13. Sterling Wortman (Rockefeller Foundation), interview, New York, March 12, 1975.

14. F.F. Hill, letter to this author, New York, March 26, 1975. Henceforth, "letter" must be taken to mean that it was addressed to this writer.

15. Sterling Wortman, "Extending the Green Revolution," *World Development*, 1, no. 12 (December 1973), 49.

16. Ibid.

17. Ibid., p. 45.

18. F.F. Hill, interview, New York, February 18, 1975.

19. Werner Kiene (Ford Foundation), interview, New York, February 19, 1975.

20. Montague Yudelman (World Bank), interview, Washington, D.C., February 24, 1975.

21. Lester R. Brown (Worldwatch Institute), interview, Washington, D.C., February 27, 1975.

22. V.W. Ruttan and Yujiro Hayami, "Technology Transfer and Agricultural Development," *Technology and Culture*, XIV, no. 2 (April 1973), 124.

23. Ibid., 141.

24. Ibid., 145–146.

25. Robert F. Chandler, Jr., "IRRI—The First Decade," in *Rice, Science and Man* (Los Banos, Philippines: International Rice Research Institute, 1972), pp. 8–9. Chandler directed IRRI from 1960 to 1972.

26. Ibid., pp. 12–15.

27. Ibid., pp. 15–16.

28. A. Colin McClung, "IRRI's Role in Institutional Cooperation in Asia," in *Rice, Science and Man* (Los Banos, Philippines: International Rice Research Institute, 1972), pp. 20–25. McClung is the associate director for agricultural sciences, Rockefeller Foundation.

29. Ibid., p. 28.

30. Ibid., pp. 28–37.

31. Burton E. Swanson, "Impact of the International System on National Research Capacity: The IRRI and CIMMYT Training Programs" (Paper prepared for the Conference on Resource Allocation and Productivity in International Agricultural Research, Airlie House, Virginia, January 26–29, 1975), p. 19.

32. Ibid., pp. 21–23, 31.

33. James M. Francen (World Bank), interview, Washington, D.C., February 26, 1975.

34. Burton E. Swanson, "Training Agricultural Research and Extension Workers from Less Developed Countries: An Examination of Training Approaches Used by the International Rice Research Institute and the International Maize and Wheat Improvement Center" (Ph.D. dissertation, University of Wisconsin, 1974), pp. 94–96.

35. Ibid., pp. 161–163.

36. Robert E. Evenson, "Comparative Evidence on Returns to Investment in National and International Research Institutions" (Paper prepared for the Conference on Resource Allocation and Productivity in International Agricultural Research, Airlie House, Virginia, January 26–29, 1975), pp. 8–9.

37. Robert E. Evenson, "Cycles in Research Productivity and International Diffusion Patterns in Sugarcane, Wheat, and Rice" (Paper prepared for the Conference on Resource Allocation and Productivity in International Agricultural Research, Airlie House, Virginia, January 26–29, 1975), p. 18.

38. Robert E. Evenson, "Comparative Evidence on Returns to Investment in National and International Research Institutions," p. 2.

39. Theodore W. Schultz, *Transforming Traditional Agriculture* (New Haven, Conn.: Yale University Press, 1964).

40. Sterling Wortman, interview, New York, February 18, 1975.

41. *CIMMYT Review 1974* (El Batan, Mexico: International Maize and Wheat Improvement Center, 1974), pp. 58–59.

42. Wortman, interview, February 18, 1975.

43. John A. Pino (Rockefeller Foundation), letter, New York, January 7, 1975.

44. Wortman, p. 45.

45. Glaucio Ary Dillon Soares, "Who Pays for Brazil's 'Economic Miracle'?" *Worldview*, 18, no. 3 (March 1975), 32.

46. Sterling Wortman, "The Technological Basis for Intensified Agricul-

ture," in *Agricultural Development: Proceedings of a Conference Sponsored by the Rockefeller Foundation* (Villa Serbelloni, Bellagio, Italy: April 23–25, 1969), p. 11.

47. Hill, interview, February 18, 1975.

48. Ralph W. Cummings, Jr. (Rockefeller Foundation), interview, New York, March 10, 1975.

49. Ruttan and Hayami, p. 121.

50. "Bellagio VI: Strengthening National Agricultural Research; Notes" (Conference, The Bellagio Study and Conference Center, Villa Serbelloni, Bellagio, Italy, March 19–21, 1974).

51. A. Colin McClung, "Strengthening National Agricultural Research Systems: Some Concerns of the International Community" (Paper, Rockefeller Foundation, c. early 1975), p. 15.

52. Wortman, "The Technological Basis for Intensified Agriculture," pp. 15–16.

53. R.G. Anderson, "Expanding the CIMMYT Outreach Programs," in *Triticale: Proceedings of an International Symposium*, edited by Reginald MacIntyre and Marilyn Campbell (El Batan, Mexico: International Development Research Centre, 1974), p. 132.

54. Wortman, "The Technological Basis for Intensified Agriculture," p. 19.

55. John W. Mellor, "Developing Science and Technology Systems— Experience and Lessons from Agriculture" (Occasional Paper no. 63, Employment and Income Distribution Project, Department of Agricultural Economics, Cornell University, May 1973), p. 8.

56. Hans W. Singer, "A New Approach to the Problems of the Dual Society in Developing Countries," *International Social Development Review*, 3 (1971), 24.

57. Lester R. Brown, *Seeds of Change: The Green Revolution and Development in the 1970's* (New York: Praeger, 1970), p. 52.

58. Robert E. Evenson, "Investment in Agricultural Research: A Survey Paper" (Paper prepared for the Consultative Group on International Agricultural Research, CG 73/4.1, October 1973), p. 4.

59. Ibid., pp. 6–7.

60. Ibid., pp. 14–16.

61. Evenson, "Comparative Evidence on Returns to Investment in National and International Research Institutions," pp. 5–7.

62. Evenson, "Cycles in Research Productivity and International Diffusion Patterns in Sugarcane, Wheat and Rice," p. 25.

63. Evenson, "Investment in Agricultural Research," p. 24.

64. McClung, "Strengthening National Agricultural Research Systems," p. 10.

65. Kiene, interview, February 19, 1975.

66. A. Colin McClung, interview, New York, March 10, 1975.

67. Lowell S. Hardin and Norman R. Collins (Ford Foundation), interview, New York, February 18, 1975.

68. Wortman, "The Technological Basis for Intensified Agriculture," p. 8.

69. John A. Pino, letter, New York, January 7, 1975.

70. Dale E. Hathaway, "Food Prices and Inflation," *Brookings Papers on Economic Activity*, 1 (1974), 76.
71. Dale E. Hathaway, interview, New York, March 11, 1975.
72. Sterling Wortman, "The Rural Development System of the People's Republic of China: Impressions and Questions" (Paper, Rockefeller Foundation, November 1974), pp. 1, 3, 16–17, 25.
73. Takashi Oka, "The Challenge of Scarcity to Individual Freedom," *The Christian Science Monitor*, February 13, 1975, p. 7.
74. Refugio I. Rochin (Department of Agricultural Economics, University of California, Davis), letter, November 5, 1975.

CHAPTER 3

1. Walter J. Broderick, *Camilo Torres: A Biography of the Priest-Guerrillero* (New York: Doubleday, 1975), pp. 57–58.
2. "Killers of Colombian Indians Lose Appeal Against Jailing," *The New York Times*, June 28, 1975, p. 8.
3. Ibid., p. 13.
4. Dragoslav Avramovic et al., *Economic Growth of Colombia: Problems and Prospects* (Baltimore: The Johns Hopkins University Press, 1972), p. 9.
5. Solon Barraclough, *Agrarian Structure in Latin America* (Lexington, Mass.: Lexington Books, 1973), p. 176.
6. Avramovic et al., p. 238.
7. A. Eugene Havens and William L. Flinn, "Diffusion of Agricultural Innovations as a Factor of Social Change," in *Internal Colonialism and Structural Change in Colombia*, edited by A. Eugene Havens and William L. Flinn (New York: Praeger, 1970), p. 27.
8. Avramovic et al., p. 256.
9. Barraclough, pp. 180–184.
10. Thomas Y. Canby, "Can the World Feed Its People?" *National Geographic*, 148, no. 1 (July 1975), 22.
11. Harry Walters, "Difficult Issues Underlying Food Problems," *Science*, 188, no. 4188 (May 6, 1975), 530.
12. Refugio I. Rochin and Diego R. Londoño, "Structural Characteristics of Garcia Rovira, Colombia: Problems of Integrated Rural Development" (Paper, Rural Development Workshop, University of California, Berkeley, June 18–20, 1975).
13. Ibid., p. 32.
14. Chris O. Andrew, "The Role of Agricultural Economics in ICA" (Memorandum to Rafael Samper, Manual Rincón, Mario Valderrama, Peter Hildebrand, and James Driscoll, August 6, 1969), pp. 1–2.
15. Interview, Bogotá, August 18, 1975.
16. Julio Alberto Assís O., extensive conversations and special document prepared at the request of this writer: "Algunos de los principales problemas que se tienen para llevar a efecto la labor de desarrollo rural en el proyecto de 'Garcia Rovira,'" Málaga, August 9, 1975.

17. Eduardo Alvarez-Luna, deputy director general, CIAT, interview, August 14, 1975.

18. Interview, CIAT, Cali, Colombia, August 13, 1975.

19. This point was contested by various ICA agronomists.

20. Interview, Mondomo, near Santader de Quilichao (Cauca), Colombia, August 15, 1975.

21. Interview, August 9, 1975.

22. In August 1975 the official exchange rate for the Colombian peso was about 31 pesos to a dollar.

23. Interview, August 7, 1975.

24. Salamón Kalmanovitz, "La agricultura en Colombia 1950-1970," *Boletín Mensual de Estadística,* DANE, no. 278 (September 1974), 127, cited in Juan Enrique Araya et al., *La politica agraria en Colombia 1950–1970* (Bogotá: Fundacion para la Education Superior y el Desarrollo, 1975), p. 26.

25. P. Spijkers, interview, August 12, 1975, CIAT, Cali, Colombia. Spijkers is a FAO rural sociologist who was "imposed" on CIAT.

26. Unpublished document made available to this writer by Angel Maria Rodriquez, INCORA, Bogotá, Colombia, August 18, 1975.

CHAPTER 4

1. Robert Katz, *A Giant in the Earth* (New York: Stein and Day, 1973), p. 143.

2. Emma Rothschild, "World Food Economy," *The New Yorker*, May 26, 1975, p. 40.

3. Amulya Kumar N. Reddy, "Is Indian Science Truly Indian?" *Science Today*, January 1974, p. 13.

4. Ibid., p. 19.

5. Interview, Bogotá, Colombia, August 18, 1975.

6. Interview, Cali, Colombia, August 16, 1975.

7. Gordon Williamson, IBM, New York, telephone communication, September 2, 1975.

8. The inspector general of the Colombian Army, General Ramón Rincón Quiñones, was assassinated in the streets of Bogotá. No doubt his murder was a result of "his vigorous pursuit of guerillas in Northern Colombia." This, according to *The New York Times* (September 12, 1975, p. 30), "is a grim reminder that both urban and rural terrorism persist in this important Andean country despite the imposition of modified martial law."

9. It is interesting to note that at this moment Colombia has a Plan for Food and Nutrition: "The Colombian Government is counting on this plan to produce about $120 million of World and Inter-American Bank money. The plan would incorporate ICA, INCORA, CAJA AGRARIA [Agrarian Bank] and several other institutions under a national committee to address the problems of producing more basic staples on small farms. Supposedly, some of the increased food would be purchased by the Government and channelled to pregnant women and children (from birth to 3 years of age) in the larger cities. The idea is that children will develop expanded mental and physical abilities if well-fed from the time they are conceived. The plan is seen by [the] Colombian

elites as the best way for the country to redistribute income and basic resources to a multitude of people. Even though it is hard to imagine the plan
actually working, it is a plan expressing a national commitment to solve some
of the problems of the poor." Refugio I. Rochin, letter, Davis, California,
November 5, 1975.

CHAPTER 5

1. "Bangladesh Land, Water and Power Studies: Final Report" (Paper,
Harvard University: Center for Population Studies, June 1972), ch. VI, pp. 2,
15–20.
2. Takashi Oka, "The Long-term Pull Needed to Avert Starvation," *The
Christian Science Monitor*, February 11, 1975, p. 7.
3. Morris Singer, *Growth, Equality and the Mexican Experience* (Austin:
University of Texas Press, 1969), p. 49.
4. Barbara H. Tuckman, "The Green Revolution, Agricultural Productivity and the Income Distribution in Mexico" (Ph.D. dissertation, The Florida
State University, 1974), pp. 24–25.
5. Clark W. Reynolds, *The Mexican Economy, Twentieth Century Structure and Growth* (New Haven: Yale University Press, 1970), p. 300.
6. Pierre R. Crosson (Resources for the Future), interview, Washington,
D.C., February 28, 1975.
7. Tuckman, pp. 28–29.
8. Ibid., pp. 154–157.
9. Werner Kiene, interview, New York, February 19, 1975.
10. Peter R. Jennings (International Center for Tropical Agriculture), letter, Cali, Colombia, January 22, 1975.
11. Solon Barraclough and Jacobo Schatan, "Technological Policy and Agricultural Development," *Land Economics*, XLIX, no. 2 (May 1973), 177–178.
12. Ibid., pp. 180–181.
13. Ibid., p. 181.
14. Ibid.
15. Ibid., p. 175.
16. Pieter Lieftinck et al., *Water and Power Resources of West Pakistan*, 3
vols. (Baltimore: The Johns Hopkins Press, 1968–1969), I, 223.
17. Ibid., II, 239.
18. Ibid., I, 18.
19. Ibid., I, 20.
20. Ibid., I, 73–74.
21. Ibid., II, 240.
22. Sudhir Sen, *A Richer Harvest: New Horizons for Developing Countries*
(New York: Orbis Books, 1974), p. 476.
23. Shyamal Roy, "Effects of Farm Tractorization on Productivity and
Labor Employment on Punjab Farms, India" (Ph.D. dissertation, University of
Missouri, 1974), pp. 1–3.
24. Ibid., pp. 3–5.
25. Ibid., p. 84.
26. Ibid., pp. 87–89.

27. "Bangladesh Land, Water and Power Studies," Chapter VI, p. 28.

28. John W. Mellor, "Relating Research Resource Allocation to Multiple Goals" (Paper prepared for the Conference on Resource Allocation and Productivity in International Agricultural Research, Airlie House, Virginia, January 26–29, 1975), p. 6a.

29. Ibid., p. 22.

30. John W. Mellor and Uma J. Lele, "Growth Linkages of the New Food-grain Technologies," *Indian Journal of Agricultural Economics,* XXVIII, no. 1 (January-March 1973), cited in Ibid., p. 1.

31. Fred Sanderson (Brookings Institution), interview, Washington, D.C., February 26, 1975.

32. The International Rice Research Institute, "Constraints on Rice Production," in "Internal Program Review" (Unpublished document, Rockefeller Foundation, February 1, 1974), pp. 1–2.

33. F.F. Hill, interview, New York, February 18, 1975.

34. Gunnar Myrdal, "On Reforming Economic Aid," *Center Report,* VIII, no. 1 (February 1975), 3.

35. Dale E. Hathaway and Swati Desai, "The Food, Agricultural and Income Situation in Asia and Pacific Region" (Paper, Ford Foundation, c. late 1974–early 1975), p. 6.

CHAPTER 6

1. Consultative Group on International Agricultural Research, Technical Advisory Committee, *Priorities for International Support to Agricultural Research in Developing Countries* (Rome: TAC Secretariat, Food and Agriculture Organization of the United Nations, 1973), pp. 1–2.

2. Ibid., p. 3.

3. Ibid.

4. Ibid., p. 4.

5. Lowell S. Hardin and Norman R. Collins, "International Agricultural Research: Organizing Themes and Issues," *Agricultural Administration,* 1 (1974), 18.

6. *Priorities for International Support to Agricultural Research in Developing Countries,* p. 7.

7. Ibid., p. 8.

8. Hardin and Collins, p. 18.

9. Ibid., p. 19.

10. *Priorities for International Support to Agricultural Research in Developing Countries,* p. 12.

11. V.E. Gracen (Department of Plant Breeding and Biometry, Cornell University), letter, Ithaca, N.Y., March 3, 1975.

12. *Priorities for International Support to Agricultural Research in Developing Countries,* p. 11.

13. John Steinhart, in *Workshop on Research Methodologies for Studies of Energy, Food, Man and Environment,* prepared by David Pimentel et al., Phase II (Ithaca, N.Y.: Cornell University, Center for Environmental Quality Management, November 11, 1974), p. 2.

14. V. Cervinka, in Ibid., p. 5.
15. Cervinka, in Ibid., pp. 5, 9.
16. *Workshop on Research Methodologies for Studies of Energy, Food, Man and Environment*, p. 14.
17. Richard Levins, "Genetics and Hunger," *Genetics*, 78, no. 1 (September 1974), 67.
18. Ibid.
19. Ibid., p. 68.
20. Gregor Johann Mendel (1822–1884) was an Austrian Augustinian monk. After eight years of experiments with peas he concluded that heredity was definitely different from variation. Heredity comes in units, not in blendings. Mathematical biology began with Mendel.
21. Levins, pp. 68–69.
22. Ibid., p. 69.
23. Ibid., p. 71.
24. Ibid., pp. 75–76.

CHAPTER 7

1. Gunnar Myrdal, "On Reforming Economic Aid," *Center Report*, VIII, no. 1 (February 1975), 5.
2. Robert S. McNamara, "Greening the Landscape," *Saturday Review/World*, December 14, 1974, p. 24.
3. Sudhir Sen, *A Richer Harvest: New Horizons for Developing Countries* (New York: Orbis Books, 1974), p. 483.
4. Jean Mayer, "The Roots of the Food Crisis" (Paper, Harvard University, School of Public Health, early 1975), p. 11. A summary of this essay appeared in the *Reader's Digest*, May 1975.
5. André Mayer and Jean Mayer, "Agriculture, The Island Empire," *Daedalus*, 103, no. 3 (Summer 1974), 86.
6. Jean Mayer (School of Public Health, Harvard University), interview, Boston, February 14, 1975.
7. Jean Mayer, "Let Us Give Aid—With Strings Attached" (Paper, Harvard University, School of Public Health, early 1975), p. 2. A summary of this essay appeared in the *Reader's Digest*, September 1975.
8. Jean Mayer, "The Roots of the Food Crisis," p. 14.
9. *The New Republic*, November 30, 1974, p. 4.
10. Laurence I. Hewes, Jr., "U.S. Short Term Food Policy Alternatives," *Center Report*, VIII, no. 2 (April 1975), 9.
11. Sterling Wortman, "World Food Needs and Opportunities: The Overview" (Paper delivered at the 66th Annual Meeting of the American Society of Agronomy, Special Session, Chicago, November 12, 1974), p. 6; Lester R. Brown and Erik P. Eckholm, *By Bread Alone* (New York: Praeger, 1974), p. 230.
12. Wortman, "World Food Needs and Opportunities," p. 12.
13. Anthony Lewis, "Heat in the Kitchen," *The New York Times*, March 6, 1975, p. 37. See also Wade Greene, "Triage: Who Shall Be Fed? Who Shall Starve?" *The New York Times Magazine*, January 5, 1975, p. 45.

CONCLUSION

1. John D. Montgomery, *Technology and Civic Life: Making and Implementing Development Decisions* (Cambridge, Mass.: The MIT Press, 1974), pp. 230–231.

2. Andrew Pearse et al., *The Social and Economic Implications of Large-Scale Introduction of New Varieties of Foodgrain* (Geneva: United Nations Research Institute for Social Development, 1974), pp. 4–5.

3. "Madras Is Reaping a Bitter Harvest of Rural Terrorism," *The New York Times*, January 15, 1969, p. 12.

4. Richard Levins, letter, Chicago, February 11, 1975.

5. Robert S. McNamara, *Address to the Board of Governors* (Washington, D.C.: International Bank for Reconstruction and Development, September 1, 1975), pp. 17–18.

6. Hesiod, *Works and Days*, in *Greek Verse*, edited by Constantine A. Trypanis (Baltimore: Penquin Books, 1971), pp. 107–109.

7. Robert S. McNamara, "Greening the Landscape," *Saturday Review/World*, December 14, 1974, p. 23.

8. Gunnar Myrdal, *Against the Stream: Critical Essays on Economics* (New York: Vintage Books, 1975), pp. 104–105.

9. Keith Griffin, *The Political Economy of Agrarian Change: An Essay on the Green Revolution* (Cambridge, Mass.: Harvard University Press, 1974), pp. 254–255.

10. Solon L. Barraclough, "Politics First," *Ceres*, 7, no. 5 (September-October 1974), 28.

11. Ibid.

12. André Mayer and Jean Mayer, "Agriculture, The Island Empire," *Daedalus*, 103, no. 3 (Summer 1974), 83.

13. Sterling Wortman, "World Food Needs and Opportunities: The Overview" (Paper delivered at the 66th Annual Meeting of the American Society of Aeronomy, Special Session, Chicago, November 12, 1974), p. 6.

14. Albert Szent-Gyorgyi, "Snakes do it. So Must Man," *The New York Times*, March 29, 1975, p. 23.

Index

About the Author

E.G. Vallianatos studied biology and history at the University of Illinois and Wisconsin. He then did postdoctoral studies and research at Harvard University in the history of science, resource transfers, and science and population policies. His interests in the political and social economy of the world food problem and of underdevelopment led to the writing of this book. In late 1975 he left the Harvard Center for Population Studies and joined the Office of Technology Assessment of the United States Congress.